REA

FRIENDS
OF ACPL

CAPTAIN COOK

Captain Cook (1728-1779) has inspired a ceaseless stream of biographies. R. T. Gould's, first published before the war, remains the best short summary. This new edition is edited by Gavin Kennedy, who remarks in his introduction that hardly any corrections were needed even in the light of forty years' scholarship.

Gould was uniquely suited to be Cook's biographer. He himself served in the Royal Navy from 1906 to 1915, and subsequently in the Hydrographic Department of the Admiralty, where he became skilled in chartmaking and surveying—both fields in which Cook made important scientific advances. Gould was a prolific author, both as a naval historian and as a populariser of such subjects as astronomy and geography. His lifelong interest in mechanical things, especially eighteenth-century chronometers, gave him unrivalled insight into the navigational problems faced by Cook, and he had the gift of communicating such technical details both accurately and clearly.

Gould is always fair to his subject. He does not disguise the more negative side of Cook's character – his hot temper and sometimes ruthless determination – but he does full justice to his achievements as a navigator and as an innovator in the diet and living conditions of seamen. His useful maps of the extent of the known world before and after Cook's voyages, and of the supposed southern continent of Terra Australis whose existence Cook disproved, have been redrawn for this edition.

Portrait of Captain James Cook by Nathaniel Dance, 1776.

CAPTAIN COOK

R. T. Gould

Duckworth

ALLEN COUNTY PUBLIC LIBRARY
FORT WAYNE, INDIANA

New edition with Introduction 1978
First published 1935
Gerald Duckworth & Co. Ltd
The Old Piano Factory
43 Gloucester Crescent, London NW1

Copyright © R. T. Gould
Introduction © 1978 by Gerald Duckworth & Co. Ltd.

All rights reserved. No part of this publication may be reproduced, stored in a retrieval system, or transmitted, in any form or by any means, electronic, mechanical, photocopying, recording or otherwise, without the prior permission of the publisher.

ISBN 0 7156 1061 9

Made and printed in Great Britain by
The Garden City Press Limited
Letchworth, Hertfordshire SG6 1JS

Contents

7020763

Chronology	7
Introduction by Gavin Kennedy	9
1. Early Years	15
2. How the First Voyage Came About	28
3. The First Voyage	45
4. The Second Voyage	74
5. The Last Voyage	100
6. Cook's Death – and After	117
Index	125

Chronology

1728 Birth of James Cook.
1746 Cook goes to sea in the merchant service.
1755 He volunteers into the Navy.
1757 He becomes a Master, R.N.
1760 He takes part in the capture of Quebec.
1763 Survey of Newfoundland begun.
1768 Appointed Lt.-in-command, H.M.S. *Endeavour*. Observes Transit of Venus at Tahiti. Rediscovers and entirely charts New Zealand.
1770 Discovers and charts E. coast of Australia.
1771 Returns to England after his first voyage round the world.
1772 Cook promoted to Commander. Sails with *Resolution* and *Adventure* in search of a Southern Continent.
1773 The Antarctic Circle crossed for the first time on record.
1774 Cook reaches his 'farthest south', 71° 10′ S.
1775 He rediscovers South Georgia and discovers the S. Sandwich islands. Returns to England after his second voyage round the world.
1776 Cook promoted to Captain. Sails with *Resolution* and *Discovery* in search of a N.W. or N.E. Passage.

1777 Discovers and explores many islands in S. Pacific.

1778 Cook discovers the Sandwich Islands, and explores the N.W. coast of N. America. He reaches his 'farthest north', 70° 44′ N.

1779 Cook killed at Kealakekua Bay, Hawaii.

INTRODUCTION

Gavin Kennedy

Of the hundreds of biographies of Captain James Cook, three stand out above the rest: those by Andrew Kippis, J. C. Beaglehole and Rupert Gould.

Kippis's *A Narrative of the Voyages round the World Performed by Captain James Cook with an account of his life during the previous and intervening periods* was published in 1788, nine years after Cook's death. It was a well-balanced account of Cook's life that relied on the documentary evidence available, the testimony of Cook's colleagues and contemporaries and interviews with his widow. It went through numerous editions, and is of great interest as a historical document. Apart from its unique sources, it served to keep open the question of the true circumstances of Captain Cook's death, which had been covered up by the author of the official narrative, Captain James King. King had edited Cook's journals and provided his own version of Cook's death and the voyage that followed; his account – published in 1784 – was designed to whitewash the conduct of certain of Cook's officers and also of Cook himself.

The outstanding scholarly life of Cook is J. C. Beaglehole's *The Life of Captain James Cook*. This was the culmination of forty years' work, twenty of which were spent in archival collection and study. These years produced the four-volume edition of Cook's Journals,

The Journals of Captain James Cook on his Voyages of Discovery, edited by J. C. Beaglehole and R. A. Skelton and published by the Hakluyt Society from 1955 to 1969. Beaglehole commenced his *magnum opus* in 1967 and died while it was in the press. It was published in 1974, three years after his death. On its 740 pages, cross-referenced with his edition of the journals, Beaglehole stamped his scholarship and mastery of the subject in an achievement unlikely to be superseded.

The third outstanding biography of Cook is this modest volume, written by Rupert Gould and first published in 1935. It is shorter than Kippis and Beaglehole by several hundred pages; yet on any comparison it matches them in excellence. Apart from his conciseness and meticulous approach, Gould was uniquely fitted to write the book by the circumstances of his life.

Rupert Thomas Gould was born in Portsmouth on November 16, 1890, the son of a composer. He joined the Royal Navy at sixteen from Dartmouth Royal Naval College and served in the Mediterranean, the Yangtse River in China and the Home Fleet. His naval service in the First World War ended in 1915 when he was invalided out. In 1916 he took a shore job in the Hydrographic Department, where he worked until 1927. This work gave him professional expertise in surveying, chartmaking and scientific navigation, 140 years after Captain Cook had displayed his genius as the first scientific navigator and cartographer.

Gould was passionately interested in all things mechanical, particularly the workings of eighteenth-century chronometers. In 1920 he offered to clean and reconstruct the irreplaceable Harrison chronometers. John Harrison, in 1761, had won the prize, offered by Act of Parliament, for constructing a reliable and workable chronometer. On his second voyage Cook took four chronometers with him: three made by John Arnold, which proved unsatisfactory, and one made by Larcum Kendal to Harrison's design, which did a magnificent job. Accurate time-keepers made scientific navigation possible and enabled a ship's longitude to be determined without guesswork.

The technical details need not detain us (they are discussed in the text), but we should note that it took Gould thirteen years to complete the task he set himself in 1920. This labour of love gave him more sympathy for Cook's achievements than would have been possible by any other means available to an author. An expert knowledge of eighteenth-century horological mechanisms combined with a professional competence in chartmaking made Gould an admirable biographer for Cook. The fact that they had both served in the same service was an added link.

Gould was a prolific author, and not just on nautical topics. He was also a broadcaster, serving on the BBC's pre-war Brains Trust, and he published a number of books. In 1928 appeared *Oddities: A book of unexplained facts*, which was followed in 1929 by *Enigmas: Another book of unexplained facts*. In 1934 he published a book on the Loch Ness Monster – surely a sign of the insatiable curiosity that is the hallmark of all explorers. Among nautical scholars, however, he became known for his professional contributions to naval history, in particular for his paper, published in *The Mariner's Mirror* in 1928, 'Bligh's Notes on Cook's Last Voyage' (vol. 14, no. 4, October, 1928). This short paper is cited in practically every book written since on Captain Bligh. In it, Gould brought to light evidence from the hand of Bligh that his charts and surveys had been purloined by Captain King and attributed to others. Gould had come across a copy of King's account of the third voyage in the Admiralty Library; it had been extensively annotated by Bligh, probably during his time at the Hydrographic Department in the early 1800s. Gould reproduced Bligh's comments on the origin of many of the charts and also Bligh's remarks on King's version of the events that led to Cook's death. Gould deserves much of the credit for re-opening what was until then a closed chapter in the history of that voyage. (I give a full account of Bligh's views on the death of Cook in my book *The Death of Captain Cook*, Duckworth, 1978.)

Gould completed the reconstruction of the Harrison chronometers in 1933 and they were exhibited in the National Maritime Museum. His *Captain Cook* was published two years later in Duckworth's Great Lives series. The book encapsulates in paragraph after paragraph the essential man that was Captain Cook, without sentimentality or romantic hero-worship. Gould presents Cook as he was, warts and all, and lets the work of his last ten years speak for itself on his behalf. Gould's intimate understanding of the scientific tools that Cook had with him on his second and third voyages (and of what it meant to be without them on his first), his appreciation of what Cook's discoveries did for the known map of the world and his feeling for Cook as a commander make this book beyond doubt one of the best ever written on the subject.

In preparing this second edition for publication I have found only minor errors, almost all of them typographical. It is an instructive comment on the accuracy of Gould's work that almost nothing needed correction in the light of Beaglehole's subsequent forty years of scholarship. Such precision, characteristic perhaps of a horologist, is only too rare in books on Cook.

It remains only to note that Rupert Gould went on

writing until 1947, mainly books on the wonders of the world, on popular astronomy and on matters horological and geographical. He died on October 5, 1948. The final paragraph of his *Captain Cook* is perhaps also the most fitting summary of his own life.

Edinburgh   GAVIN KENNEDY

CHAPTER ONE

Early Years

To the average man of to-day, Captain Cook is little more than a name. But he is at least that – and, if we except Christopher Columbus and the latest newspaper-hero, there is hardly any other explorer of whom as much can confidently be said. Modern exponents of 'debunking' may contend that his name is a household word because, like that of the great Genoese, it rolls trippingly off the tongue; but in sober fact he had it in him to achieve immortality under any name, and in any age.

He was at once the last of the great early navigators and the first of the modern scientific explorers. Starting life as a grocer's shop-boy, and painfully educating himself for his life-work while serving in the Navy as a warrant officer, he extended the outline of the known world as widely as ever did Columbus or Magellan; while he mapped his discoveries so accurately that, with slight modifications in detail, his charts of them might be used to-day. In fact his explorations resemble, in their technique, the brush-work of a master – a bold, sweeping outline, completed by the most delicate stippling. In their combined extent and accuracy, they have never been rivalled, and never will be: for (except in the Polar regions) Cook left the map of the world, in outline, substantially as we know it to-day.

His work as an explorer was crowded into the last ten

years of his life – ten years of wonderful achievement preceded by forty of obscure drudgery. If he had died at forty, he would only be remembered, by a few geographical students, as Michael Lane is now – as a diligent eighteenth-century surveyor who did good work in Newfoundland and Labrador. His fame rests entirely and securely upon his doings from the day he hoisted his pennant in the *Endeavour* to the day, ten years later, when he was stunned and hacked to pieces by the Hawaiians. In the years between, he made his famous 'three voyages round the world' – the first in 1768–71, the second in 1772–75, and the third in 1776–79: and the story of those three voyages is, in effect, the story of Cook's life – or, at least, of his life-work.

By comparison, the events of his previous career are like some long and rather dull prelude, which one endures in anticipation of the brilliant fugue succeeding it. Here, then, is a concise arrangement of that prelude.

James Cook was born at Marton in Cleveland, Yorkshire, on October 27, 1728. He was the second son of James and Grace Cook, to whom five girls and another son were born subsequently. His father, who was a farm-hand, was a Scot from Roxburghshire.

In 1736 the elder Cook was appointed bailiff of Airy Holme farm, near Ayton. James, who had already been taught his letters by a charitable lady at Marton, one Mrs. Walker, was sent to school at High Green, Ayton, where he learned writing and the rudiments of arithmetic. Reasonably diligent in school, he was better remembered by his school-mates for his initiative and resourcefulness in any really serious matter, such as bird-nesting. Is it a coincidence that a similar legend attaches to another boy – generally referred to at Market Drayton, about this period, as 'that young scapegrace, Bob Clive'?

At the age of thirteen or so, Cook left school to help

Early Years

his father on the farm; but in 1745 he was engaged as shop-boy by a Mr. Sanderson, a grocer at Staithes, a fishing village near Whitby. Cook was not, as is often stated, bound apprentice to Sanderson – the agreement was verbal, and could be terminated at any time by either party.

He remained in the Staithes shop for some eighteen months; but it was soon evident that, stirred by the talk of the local fishermen and coasters, he was bent on a sea life. Still, his work satisfied his master – and a persistent local tradition that he stole a shilling from the till and fled to sea is sufficiently refuted by the fact that Sanderson himself put him in the way of following his bent. He introduced him to Mr. John Walker – one of the Walkers of Whitby, a well-known firm of coal-shippers – as a likely lad for the coastal trade.

About July, 1746, Cook signed indentures binding him apprentice to Walker (personally) for three years. His first voyages were made in the *Freelove*, a collier of some 341 tons plying along the east coast; and between voyages he lodged, as was the custom, in his employer's house. It was while staying there that, so far as is known, he began to study elementary navigation – that 'art and mystery' which, for almost all seamen of his day, was and would always remain a sealed book.

After several voyages in the *Freelove*, he took part in rigging and fitting-out a new ship of Walker's, the *Three Brothers*, and he remained in her until 1750 – signing on, after his apprenticeship had expired, as an A.B. In 1750 he was in the *Mary*, trading to the Baltic; and in 1752, aged twenty-four, he was appointed mate of Messrs. Walkers' latest ship, the *Friendship*. He held this position for three years; and his employer then offered him the command.

But Cook had other plans. In June, 1755, he left his ship, then in the Thames, and volunteered into the

Royal Navy as an A.B. The only explanation he ever gave of this action was, that he had 'a mind to try his fortune that way'. What his motives were, we shall probably never know. He had given every satisfaction to the Walkers, and remained on excellent terms with them all his life – moreover, they did all that they could to recommend him for advancement in the Navy. He was under no compulsion to join it – as master of the *Friendship*, he would have been exempt from the 'hot press' then being carried on in anticipation of war with France, and if seized by a press-gang he would have been free again within forty-eight hours. Nor could he anticipate rising either fast or far in his new service. True, in the eighteenth century – as in the twentieth, but not the nineteenth – a man might rise from A.B. to Admiral; but few could hope to do this. The most that Cook could legitimately expect was, that his knowledge of navigation would soon bring him his Warrant as Master – the officer then charged with the safe-conduct of a ship when at sea.

Still, he was only twenty-seven – old enough to know his own mind, while young enough to change his way of life – he 'had a mind to try his fortune that way', and he had no ties. His father had prospered sufficiently to warrant his building, in this very year, that cottage at Ayton in which he and his wife ended their lives, and which has now been transported to Australia as a concrete – or, rather, brick – monument of their famous son.

James Cook's name makes its first appearance in the Admiralty records on the Muster Roll of H.M.S. *Eagle*, at Portsmouth. He is entered as having repaired on board of her on June 25, 1755; the date of his actual admission into the Service (at the Wapping 'rendezvous') being June 17. On the following July 24, some six weeks later, we find him rated as 'Master's mate', a

Early Years

rating which he held until he left the *Eagle* two years later.

That peculiar type, the 'Master, R.N.', began to grow definitely rare in the middle of last century, and is now quite extinct. He was a warrant officer – a man, that is, usually of humble beginnings – who had acquired some smattering of navigation. Complicated but not really abstruse, this art can be plied, while still but half-understood, by the half-educated; and in the eighteenth century it generally was. However little the Master of a king's ship might know about '. . . that excellent Art which demonstrateth by infallible conclusion how a sufficient Ship may be conducted the shortest good way from place to place . . .' his Captain probably knew less; and so long as the Master kept his ship off the ground, and 'magnified his office', he customarily passed for – and, in fact, frequently was – an able man. But his limited education made him a rule-of-thumb reef-dodger rather than a scientific navigator; and the advent of steam, by putting a premium on exact methods and clear thinking, soon pushed him out of the picture.

While Cook would have been the first to admit that his education was far from complete – even as far as concerned the special knowledge needed for his new calling – he probably knew more about navigation than most Masters then serving; and it is not in the least surprising that his special qualifications should have been at once recognised. 'Master's mate' was not a very exalted position – it was, in fact, not much higher than that of the modern 'quartermaster', who acts as helmsman or leadsman upon special occasions – but it was a promise of something better.

During the two years – the opening years of the Seven Years' War – which Cook spent in the *Eagle* he saw a good deal of fairly strenuous service, though cruising in home waters. His first captain, Hamar, incurred Their Lordship's displeasure by careening his ship at Plymouth without waiting for them to sanction this step, and he was superseded by Capt. Hugh Palliser. In afterlife, Palliser was both Cook's powerful patron and his sincere friend; but there is no evidence that, while serving together in the *Eagle*, their relations were anything more than those customary between Captain and foc'sle hand.

In April, 1756, Cook enjoyed his first taste of independent command when, in charge of an armed party, he navigated a hired cutter from the Bass Rock to Plymouth. In the following year he saw active service – the *Eagle* distinguished herself by capturing the French East-Indiaman *Duc D'Aquitaine*, in heavy weather, at the mouth of the Channel. For this action, Palliser received the thanks of the Admiralty.

Meanwhile, Cook's friends the Walkers had been doing their best to promote both him and his interests. At their suggestion Mr. Osbaldestone, M.P. for Scarborough (an ancestor of the famous 'Squire of England') asked Palliser to recommend Cook for a Lieutenant's commission; and Palliser, while replying that Cook, not having yet completed six years Naval service, was ineligible for this, intimated that he might be given a Master's warrant, '. . . by which he would be raised to a station that he was well qualified to discharge with ability and credit'. In the event, Cook was discharged from the *Eagle* on June 30, 1757, joining H.M.S. *Solebay* at Leith in Scotland on July 30 as Master.

In recording this event Cook's first biographer, Dr. Andrew Kippis, went badly astray and took several of his successors with him. He appoints him, on three consecutive days, to three different ships – the *Grampus*, then the *Garland*, and finally the *Mercury*, in which he makes him serve some months, remarking at the same time that these '. . . quick and successive appointments

Early Years

show that his interest was strong, and that the intention to serve him was real and effectual'. Actually, Cook was never in any of the three. How the mistake about the 'quick and successive appointments' to the *Grampus* and *Garland* arose, is uncertain; but his mythical appointment to the *Mercury* is simply due, as Kitson first showed in 1907, to the fact that in 1757 there were at least two Masters in the Navy named James Cook – one of them Master of the *Solebay*, the other of the *Mercury*. Kippis happened to pick the wrong one, who never rose above Lieutenant, and died in 1800. I say 'at least two', because there may have been several more (a point which Kitson overlooked). For example, in November, 1763 one 'James Cook, Master' was serving in the *Alarm*, frigate, in the West Indies. This cannot have been either the great James Cook, who was then in the *Antelope* on the Newfoundland station, or his namesake of the *Mercury*, who was then a Lieutenant in the *Hazard*.

Cook only spent about six weeks in the *Solebay*, and in consequence his signature does not appear in any of her official documents. On October 18, 1757, he was appointed to H.M.S. *Pembroke* as Master, probably through the good offices of his friend Bisset, formerly Master of the *Eagle*, who had superintended the *Pembroke*'s fitting out. He joined his new ship on his twenty-ninth birthday, October 27, 1757.

The *Pembroke* was destined to take part in one of the major operations of the war; the capture of the French colony of New France – or, in other words, the only settled portion of eighteenth-century Canada. As a unit of Boscawen's fleet, she left England in March for the preliminary attack on Louisburg (at the entrance to the Gulf of St. Lawrence). This, however, she missed by four days, having been left behind at Halifax to complete her crew, much weakened by scurvy.

After the fall of Louisburg, the *Pembroke* cruised with a detached squadron under Sir Charles Hardy to harass some of the local French settlements, and wintered at Halifax. In April of the following year Admiral Sir Charles Saunders, who had succeeded Boscawen, arrived there to take command of the fleet for the combined operations against Quebec. Meanwhile a squadron under Admiral Durell, including the *Pembroke*, was blockading the St. Lawrence entrance, and making provisional surveys.

These were badly needed. The lower reaches of the St. Lawrence are wide; but for some fifty miles below Quebec the river is much obstructed by islands and shoals. The French, naturally, had removed all available buoys and landmarks – and while some of their charts had been captured, these were of little real use. Safe navigation of the 'Traverse' and other difficult channels below Quebec called, therefore, for local knowledge – which the Masters of the squadron, undeterred by hostile action, set themselves to acquire.

By June, Saunders was off Newfoundland with 119 transports (containing Wolfe's army) and 22 men-of-war; and by the 26th the passage up the St. Lawrence had been safely accomplished and the troops disembarked on the Ile d'Orleans, opposite Quebec. After an abortive attack by French fireships, Saunders moved his fleet higher up river, into the basin, and stood by to cover the final landing. For this further surveys were necessary; and during their progress Wolfe and Cook met – Wolfe refers, in one of his despatches, to a conversation he had with Cook respecting the positions to be occupied by two vessels which it was intended to run ashore near the landing-place. This recalls the 'River Clyde' – and, in fact, the whole operation was much like the Gallipoli landing on a smaller scale, and with happier results. On the night of September 12, while

Cook was out with the *Pembroke*'s boats in the Basin, the famous landing was made, and the heights of Abraham occupied – with what result everyone knows. Quebec surrendered five days later.

Soon afterwards, the fleet – including the *Pembroke* – sailed for England; but Cook, who had definitely made his mark as a surveyor, was transferred to the *Northumberland*, one of seven ships left behind to form the new North American Squadron under Captain Lord Colville. This squadron was to winter at Halifax, and return to the St. Lawrence as soon as it was free of ice next year.

Accordingly, the end of May, 1760, found Cook once more in the Basin, surveying the St. Lawrence – a job which he did with extraordinary thoroughness. In four months he produced a chart (still extant) showing the difficult reaches through which the fleet had been so triumphantly carried in the previous summer. It was not a mere sketch-survey, such as most Masters of his day would have been quite content to produce – it was based, in great part, upon an accurate triangulation. How, in the limited time at his disposal, he could have effected this triangulation, is still somewhat of a mystery; but one which is quite overshadowed by the far greater mystery of when, and how, Cook managed to teach himself – there was no one available to teach him – his obviously considerable knowledge of marine surveying. He is known, however, to have spent his spare time during the winters of 1759 and 1760, when the *Northumberland* was at Halifax, in reading mathematics (including Euclid) and astronomy. Small wonder that, on January 19, 1761, Lord Colville should have directed the payment to Cook of £50, '... in consideration of his Indefatigable Industry in making himself Master of the Pilotage of the River Saint Lawrence'.

During the early summer of 1762 the *Northumberland*

remained at Halifax, and Cook made a thorough survey of the harbour. This period of inaction was suddenly ended in July, when a French force descended on St. John's and re-captured it. However, concerted action by Colville's squadron and the forces under Gen. Amherst (Commander-in Chief) compelled the invaders to surrender on September 18. During the operations the boats of the fleet were under the charge of the third lieutenant of H.M.S. *Gosport* — the former Master of the *Mercury* – and the namesakes undoubtedly met then, if not earlier.

The season, and the *Northumberland*'s commission, were drawing to a close; but Cook found time, before his ship left for England, to make two more small surveys, of Harbour Grace and Carbonera Bay. On October 24 the ship reached Spithead; and on November 11 Cook was discharged to shore, taking with him a balance of £291 19*s*. 3*d*. pay due for the commission, and a letter from Colville addressed to the Admiralty, informing them that '... from my Experience of Mr. Cook's Genius and Capacity, I think him well qualified for the Work he has performed and for greater Undertakings of the same kind'.

One greater undertaking engaged Cook's immediate attention. He took lodgings in Shadwell, and there made the acquaintance of a Miss Elizabeth Batts, aged twenty-one (he was thirty-four). They were married at St. Margaret's, Barking, a few weeks later – December 21, 1762.

Cook's married life was destined to be interrupted, by force of circumstances, for years at a time, and little is known of its details – but (possibly for that reason) it seems to have been a very happy one. Certainly he was a good husband – in after years, his wife was accustomed to regard his conduct as her unvarying standard of what was good and right. And she herself seems to have been

Early Years

much above the average – it was a union of two exceptional people, well fitted to be mates.

As Cook may have known when contemplating marriage, he was not to be idle for long. Peace with France came in February of 1763; and immediately afterwards the Governor of Newfoundland, Capt. Graves, R.N., who found his territory considerably and permanently swollen by the spoils of war, applied to the Board of Trade for permission (and funds) to employ a surveyor in charting them. The Board concurred – and Graves, who had seen something of Cook's work, and knew its worth, at once secured his services. Orders from the Admiralty, dated April 19, directed Cook to take passage in Graves's ship, the *Antelope*, to Newfoundland, '... in order to your taking a Survey of Part of the Coast and Harbours of that Island'. While so employed he was to be allowed 10*s.* a day, and the services of an assistant.

His first job was to make a rapid survey of St. Pierre and Miquelon – which, although for the moment in English hands, were due to be returned to France under the Treaty of Paris. Unfortunately, the French envoy reached the islands on the same day as the new surveyor; but the formalities attending the transfer were carefully spun out until Cook, working at high pressure, had practically finished his work. Thereafter, he began a series of coastal surveys in Newfoundland, designed to cover areas which the Admiralty regarded as of principal importance. With his assistant Smart, he returned to England in H.M.S. *Tweed* for the winter. His first son, James, was then about seven weeks old.

Early in the following year Palliser, his former captain in the *Eagle*, succeeded Graves as Governor of Newfoundland, and put the survey upon a new footing. In the previous season a small schooner, the *Grenville*, belonging to the station, had been allotted to the surveyor's use, being manned from the squadron and laid up at St. John's for the winter. Palliser induced the Navy Board to 'establish' her (that is, to put her in regular commission, with a permanent crew borne on her own books), Cook, of course, being in command. She could then be navigated to England each winter for refit, and sent over again in the spring.

Accordingly, Cook and his men left England in the *Lark*, commissioned the *Grenville* on June 14, 1764, and at once sailed to carry on the survey. The commission began somewhat ominously for Cook; on August 5, his right hand was seriously injured, and scarred for life, by the explosion of a powder-horn he was holding. In the days of flint-lock muzzle-loaders, such accidents were not uncommon, and often fatal. Early in September, too, he was nearly drowned (he could not swim, and never learned) off Ferrol point, St. John's.

From 1764 to 1768 Cook continued his survey, wintering in England each year, and returning in the spring. In other ways, too, he showed himself diligent and methodical – a second son (Nathaniel) was born to him in 1764, a daughter (Elizabeth) in 1766, and a third son (Joseph – died aged one month) in 1768. But the most important event of this period, so far as it ultimately affected Cook's own fortunes, was a piece of scientific work, outside the ordinary run of his duties, which he performed in 1766. On August 5, there was an eclipse of the sun, which was very carefully observed by Cook from the Burgeo Is., near Cape Ray. Similar good observations had been secured at Greenwich – and on his return to England at the end of the year Cook combined the two sets and deduced the longitude of his observation-spot. It may be noted that in those days eclipses, occultations, and similar phenomena were the only means open to surveyors for determining fundamental longitudes. Hence Cook deemed his result sufficiently important to merit the attention of the Royal

Society, and accordingly communicated it to Dr. John Bevis, F.R.S., a well-known amateur astronomer. It was published in the 'Philosophical Transactions', 1767, and had far-reaching consequences.

By the end of the 1767 season, Cook had completed the survey of the W. coast of Newfoundland, and carried that of the S. coast as far as C. Chapeau Rouge. Moreover, he had prepared many of his charts for publication – in fact, one or two had already appeared in 1766. Palliser, who had learned to appreciate him during the four years of the survey, now secured Their Lordships' permission for the publication of the rest. In those days, it should be remembered, there was no Hydrographic Department, but there were many private firms of chart-publishers; and it was to the interest of all – Admiralty, publisher, surveyor, and purchaser – that a surveyor should be permitted to dispose of his work in the only market available.

How good Cook's Newfoundland charts were may be judged by the fact that they were superseded by later surveys of comparable extent only in the 1930s. They were based on an extensive triangulation, made with good instruments – Cook is known to have had a theodolite, and his quadrant, as appears from his eclipse paper, was one of Bird's best, with a brass frame and a telescope. Probably no living surveyor possessed better instruments, or better understanding of their use.

But by the time that the charts appeared, Cook's connection with the Newfoundland survey, and his service afloat as a Master R.N., had terminated for ever. On April 12, 1768, his assistant, Michael Lane, was appointed as '. . . Master of the brig *Grenville*, and the surveyor of the coasts of Newfoundland and Labrador in the absence of Mr. Cook, who is to be employed elsewhere'. The stage was set for the first of the three great voyages. The man was ready, and the hour had struck.

CHAPTER TWO

How the First Voyage Came About

Cook's first voyage round the world was brought about by a peculiar combination of causes. Originally planned as a purely astronomical expedition, it recommended itself to the Government on quite other grounds – the geographical discoveries which might ensue, and the political advantages which such discoveries would entail. These different aspects of the voyage are all important enough to require discussion.

Astronomically considered, the sole object of the voyage was to transport qualified persons to some suitable station in the South Pacific from which they could observe the Transit of Venus which was due to occur on June 3, 1769.

Some fifty years earlier, in 1716, Edmund Halley (afterwards Astronomer Royal) had pointed out, in a paper read before the Royal Society, that the eighteenth century would witness a Transit of Venus, in 1761; that such a phenomenon might recur in 1769, but would certainly not be seen thereafter until 1874; and that, by observing the whole duration of such transits from two stations differing widely in latitude, a solution could be found for the most fundamental problem which then confronted astronomers – the determination of the earth's distance from the sun. Confining himself chiefly to discussing arrangements for the Transit of 1761 – which he knew that he could no more hope to see than the

How the First Voyage Came About

return (which he successfully predicted) of his famous comet in 1758 – he suggested that observers should occupy various stations, such as Benkulen (in Sumatra) and the shores of Hudson Bay, which seemed well adapted to his method (now called 'Halley's method'). The conclusion of his exordium is worth quoting:

> I could wish that many observations of this famous phenomenon might be taken by different persons at separate places, both that we might arrive at a greater degree of certainty by their agreement, and also lest any single observer should be deprived, by the intervention of clouds, of a sight which I know not whether any man living in this or the next age will ever see again, and on which depends the certain and adequate solution of a problem the most noble, and at other times not to be attained to. I recommend it therefore again and again to those curious astronomers who, when I am dead, will have an opportunity of observing these things, that they would remember this my admonition . . . and I earnestly wish them all imaginable success.

In 1742 Halley was laid to rest in Lee churchyard; on Christmas Day, 1758, his comet reappeared; and on June 3, 1761, Venus was duly seen creeping across the face of the sun in the form of a small black dot. But while his prediction had been accurate enough in the main, it failed – as later astronomers had anticipated – in detail. His method and his station proved ill-suited to this particular occasion. However, with fine official pertinacity, English observers were despatched to Benkulen – and others would probably have also been sent to Hudson Bay if definite proof had not been forthcoming that the Transit would not be visible there at all. Luckily, the ship bound for Benkulen was forced to put in at the Cape, where excellent observations were secured; these being combined with those taken elsewhere on 'Delisle's method', which used pairs of stations differing widely in longitude.

Owing, however, to the formidable difficulties which then stood in the way of ascertaining longitudes accurately, the 1761 observations did not determine the sun's distance with any great precision; on the other hand they demonstrated (Halley had only surmised) that there would unquestionably be another Transit in 1769 – after which there would be none for more than a century. Furthermore, at this second transit the easier method – Halley's – would be available *if suitable stations could be found.*

The selection of a northern station presented no difficulty. The Transit would occur in June, when the north pole of the earth is bowed towards the sun; an observer anywhere inside the Arctic Circle could therefore, given fine weather, have the sun continuously in view day and night. But at the southern station it was necessary that the sun should be at least visible – and, preferably, well above the horizon – for the whole duration of the Transit (some six hours). In the circumstances of the case, this meant that the station should be on, or fairly near, the meridian of 155° W.; and calculations made by Maskelyne, the Astronomer Royal, indicated that it ought to lie within an area bounded by lines joining the following points; 5° S., 173° E. – 5° S., 124° W. – 35° S., 139° W. – 35° s., 172° W. (see Fig. 1).

Here, the astronomical interest of the proposed voyage gives place to the geographical. If a suitable station for observing the Transit of 1769 could be found, its occupation promised to solve a fundamental problem of geography as well as of astronomy. Not only would it help to determine the earth's distance from the sun; it

How the First Voyage Came About

could scarcely fail to throw much light on the much-agitated question of the Great Southern Continent. That an Antarctic Continent does, in fact, exist, is a commonplace of modern geography – but it is comparatively small, barren, and generally uninhabitable. Eighteenth-century geographers, however, following Ptolemy and his medieval successors, inclined to believe in the existence of a vastly different Southern Continent – one as big as Europe and Asia combined, lying mainly in the southern temperate zone and extending northward, at various points, almost into the tropics. Many of them made this almost an article of faith – although, as in all matters of faith, definite proof was lacking. Certainly in 1768 there was room for such a continent. No vessel had yet crossed, or even approached, the Antarctic Circle (66° 33' S.); 50° S. had only been reached by vessels rounding the Horn or running to the eastward of it; and over a very considerable expanse in the S. Pacific the parallel of 30° S. – more than 4,000 statute miles from the South Pole – had never been attained by any vessel.

Moreover, great stress was laid upon the supposed necessity for an enormous land-mass in the unknown regions of the south to 'balance' the apparent preponderance of land northward of the equator. Actually, this argument was a pure fallacy, and those who employed it showed a defective sense of proportion. On a globe two feet in diameter, the average height (to scale) of the various continents above sea-level does not exceed the thickness of a coat of paint; the world would be no more 'unbalanced' by having more land above sea-level in the northern hemisphere, than a tennis-ball becomes 'unbalanced' when you stencil your initials on one side of it. And even if the earth were egg-shaped – or tetrahedral, as Lowthian-Green and others have suggested – it would still revolve round its centre of gravity (as that, in turn, would around the sun) with perfect steadiness, despite its lack of 'balance'.

Needless to say, geographers who believed in the Great Southern Continent caught eagerly at any reported sighting of land in the south – provided that it had not been definitely circumnavigated – as a cape, or at least a peninsula, of their imaginary mainland. Particularly was this the case in the Southern Pacific – then more generally termed the 'Southern Ocean' – where, as already noted, there was room for a vast stretch of undiscovered coastline in quite low latitudes. Such was the view of De Brosse, D'Apres de Mannevillette, Buache, and other geographers; while no one championed it more single-mindedly than Alexander Dalrymple – who requires more than passing mention.

Dalrymple was a Scotsman, a brother of Lord Hailes, and had spent many years in the East India Company's service. At the age of twenty-five he had commanded a ship in eastern waters – while he had found time, in the intervals of his official duties, to acquire a competent knowledge of surveying and to accumulate much information respecting the early exploration of the Pacific. He was also an astronomer of some note, and an F.R.S. In character, he appears to have been a man of great ability and domineering personality – strict to the last degree with his subordinates, stubborn and unconciliating towards his superiors. His reason, though powerful, seems always to have been the slave of his prejudices; and his style (he was a voluminous writer) exactly typifies the man – vigorous, overbearing, capable, intolerant and liable, at the slightest irritation, to burst out into an eruption of italics.

At this period (1767), while still only thirty, he had temporarily returned from the east and settled in London, where he devoted much of his time to geographical research. He had just printed, but not yet published, a

How the First Voyage Came About

pamphlet, 'Discoveries in the South Pacific to 1764', in which he stoutly maintained that, in the Pacific, '... the space unknown from the Tropics to 50° S. *must* be nearly all land'. He seems to have visualised a continental mass filling the whole South Pacific from about 90° W. to 170° E., and from about 28° S. to the pole – the known outline of Tasman's 'Nieuw Zeeland' forming its western boundary, and the (non-existent) lands reported by Quiros and Davis, together with others yet to be discovered, its northern coast-line; while to the eastward its outline ran through two (equally mythical) landfalls attributed respectively to Juan Fernandez (date uncertain) and the Dutch ship *Orange Tree* (1624) (see Fig. 1).

His views were, of course, well known to the Royal Society – which, at the moment, was anxious to take the best available advice regarding the selection of a southern observing station somewhere within Maskelyne's limits. True, that authority had delimited an area considerably larger than Europe – but within it only two small groups of islands were definitely known to exist; the Marquesas in the N.E., and Amsterdam and Rotterdam near the western limit. Owing to the practical impossibility of determining longitude at sea, the exact situation of both groups was distinctly uncertain; moreover, they had never been re-visited since their discovery – by Mendana (1595) and Tasman (1643) respectively. On the other hand, nearly a quarter of the area *might* be occupied by some portion of Dalrymple's continent.

Dalrymple was ready – in fact, eager – to tender advice on the selection of a station; advice which, from the attention he had given the subject, was certain to carry great weight. Independently of this, he was a surveyor, a cartographer and a practised astronomer – and, still more to the point, he had commanded vessels sailing in eastern waters. The Royal Society must have felt a double burden lifted from their shoulders. Here was a man fully competent to select their southern station, to conduct a ship thither, and to take the necessary observations – in fact, the natural and obvious leader of their expedition.

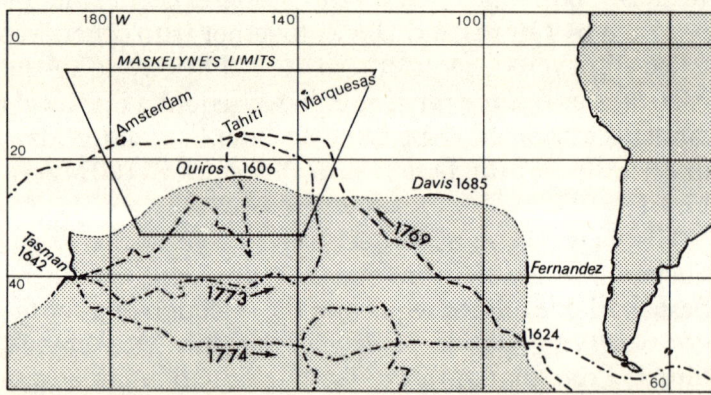

Fig. 1. The Pacific portion of the 'Great Southern Continent' as imagined by A. Dalrymple, F.R.S., about 1764: and Cook's tracks over it.

The expedition, however, was still only in embryo. The Society must provide personnel, equipment and, most important of all, a ship. Its funds were quite insufficient to buy, or even charter, one. Consequently, recourse must be had to the Admiralty – and here we come to the third motive for the voyage; its political aspect.

The Seven Years' War had seen England acquiring new territories right and left, at the expense of France and Spain. Some of these had been given back under the Treaty of Paris – some had not. We had returned Martinique to France, and Cuba and the Philippines to Spain (in exchange for Florida); but we retained the former French possessions in India and Canada. And a new spirit of expansion and colonisation was abroad – impelling England to hold, and extend, what she had won; stimulating France, and even Spain, to replace what they had lost. What was more natural than that all three should turn their attention to the unknown South Pacific – the one region where it was possible, and even likely, that extensive territories, in a temperate climate, might be had for the finding?

It is, at any rate, significant that soon after the Treaty of Paris was signed the Admiralty despatched Commodore Byron, in the *Dolphin*, with secret instructions to take formal possession of the Falkland Islands and then explore the 'South Seas', making such 'discoveries and observations' as he should find possible. But 'Foul Weather Jack Byron' lived up to his nickname; and a combination of bad weather, scurvy and ill-luck resulted in his adding practically nothing to comtemporary knowledge of the South Pacific. However, three months after his return the *Dolphin*, under Capt. Wallis, accompanied by the *Swallow*, Capt. Carteret, had been despatched with similar orders to prosecute discoveries in the South Seas – and the Admiralty were even then waiting for news of their doings.

The Royal Society, therefore, must have felt that all was more or less plain sailing. There could be little doubt that the Government would welcome an expedition which, however dimly they might apprehend its main scientific object, at least promised an excellent opportunity for taking formal possession of new lands. They were, therefore, sure of the use of a King's ship; and, not improbably, the Treasury might be induced to provide funds for the incidental expenses – or, if not, the King's keen interest in geography and astronomy might be turned to profitable account. Moreover, they had the right man for the command of the expedition. But here an unforeseen difficulty arose.

No one – at least, no one outside the Admiralty – seriously doubted that Dalrymple, in addition to directing the scientific work of the expedition, was perfectly competent to take command of any ship the Admiralty might put at the Society's disposal. But he was not, and never had been, a Naval officer; and, which was almost as important, he had been, and still was, in the service of the East India Company. On both counts – especially, I think, the latter – it was reasonable to suppose that whatever the Admiralty could do to prevent his commanding the ship would most assuredly be done – and, as it happened, they had a most efficient stumbling-block which needed very little pushing into place.

There was a precedent for Dalrymple's appointment – and a bad one. In 1699 Halley had been temporarily invested with a Captain's commission and given command of H.M. pink *Paramour* for the purpose of making magnetic observations in the South Atlantic. There had been a mutiny, and a court-martial. His First Lieutenant, irritated beyond endurance by the interference of a makee-learn Captain, had flouted his authority and been dismissed the service. Even if the Admiralty had been well disposed towards Dalrymple's appointment – and it is quite certain that they were against it from the first – they could scarcely have turned a blind eye to what had happened, in very similar circumstances, some seventy years earlier.

In any event the First Lord of the Admiralty – Hawke, the victor of Quiberon Bay – took a strong line. He swore roundly that, sooner than sign a Captain's commission for a man who was not a King's officer, he would cut his hand off. Dalrymple, possessed of even greater obstinacy, retorted that he would go in no other capacity.

The Royal Society were now in a quandary. The

How the First Voyage Came About

leader they had always had in mind was, quite obviously, *persona non grata* to the Admiralty. They must either get a ship elsewhere, or find a naval officer to lead the expedition. Possibly they may have tried – it is almost certain that Dalrymple tried – to induce the East India Company to lend a ship; but if they did, they were unsuccessful. In April, 1768 they accepted the Admiralty veto, and jettisoned Dalrymple. Somewhat curiously, the latter came within measurable distance of getting a well-paid Admiralty position some eighteen months afterwards. He was offered, and provisionally accepted, the post (not then established) of Hydrographer to the Admiralty, at £500 a year. Actually, the scheme fell through for the time; but he became the first holder of the title in 1795.

The Royal Society had discarded Dalrymple, as leader, in favour of James Cook. He was in England; he was well known as a surveyor; he had been in command of a ship for some years past; he could be spared from the Newfoundland survey; he was obviously a competent observer, as witness his eclipse paper, printed in the 'Transactions'; the Admiralty were willing to appoint him to command the ship they would provide; and he was ready and eager to accept the appointment. At the same time, the Society had reason to anticipate that the King would make a grant from the Privy Purse to cover the expenses of the expedition.

The period of lobbying being over, that of official action began. At a meeting of the Royal Society on March 24, 1768, the President (Lord Morton) announced that the King had placed a grant of £4,000, the estimated cost of the expedition, at the Society's disposal. On the 29th of that month the Admiralty's *alter ego*, the Navy Board, informed the Secretary of the Admiralty that they had purchased '... a cat-built Bark, in Burthen 368 Tuns and of the age of three years and nine months, for conveying such persons as shall be thought proper to the Southward . . .'. On April 12, as we have seen, Lane was appointed to relieve Cook in the *Grenville*. And on May 5 Cook made his first formal appearance before the R.S. Council.

He impressed them very favourably. Verging on forty, he was in his prime both physically and mentally. Spare and weathered, he stood more than six feet, with a small, well-shaped head and a most expressive face. Normally, his prominent eyebrows and keen eyes made him look stern; but in conversation his face would quickly light up – and five minutes of his company was more than enough to reveal that he was both highly intelligent and firm of purpose: a rare combination of the thinker and the man of action.

Incidentally, he was not to be 'Mr. Cook, the surveyor', much longer. He knew that he would very shortly be appointed to command the 'cat-built Bark' – the immortal *Endeavour* – and that with the appointment would come his commission as Lieutenant. He had quitted the navigating branch of the service – that blind-alley which not one Master in a thousand ever left, and in which none could ever rise higher – for good and all. His foot was on the ladder; and while no one, least of all himself, could then have foreseen how far he would go, all could appreciate that here was a man who – if appearances and merit counted for anything – was capable of great things, and who held a magnificent opportunity for doing them safely within his grasp.

The Council invited him to become one of the two southern observers of the Transit. This he at once accepted, in consideration of such a gratuity as the Society might think he deserved, and an allowance of £120 a year 'for victualling himself and another observer'. His colleague (who also attended the Council

How the First Voyage Came About

meeting) was to be Charles Green, then Maskelyne's assistant at the Royal Observatory. The Society undertook to provide them both with all necessary instruments.

Three weeks later (May 26, 1768) Cook's commission was signed, and on May 27 he hoisted his pennant in the *Endeavour* at Deptford, where she was preparing for sea.

His new command – known officially as the *Endeavour Bark* to distinguish her from another King's ship of the same name – had been built by Messrs. Fishburn of Whitby, for the coal-trade. Cook had spent several years in ships of her type, and there is little doubt that he was mainly responsible for inducing the Admiralty to order her purchase, and to reject the two King's ships, the *Tryal* and *Rose*, which the Navy Board had previously suggested as suitable for the voyage. As he wrote, long afterwards:

> A ship of this kind must not be of a great draught of water, yet of a sufficient burden and capacity to carry a proper quantity of provisions and necessaries for her complement of men, and for the term requisite to perform the voyage. She must also be of a construction that will bear to take the ground, and of a size which, in case of necessity, may be safely and conveniently laid on shore to repair any accidental damage or defect. These properties are not to be found in ships of war of forty guns, nor in frigates, nor in East India Company's ships, nor in large three-decked West India ships, nor indeed in any other but North-country ships such as are built for the coal trade, which are peculiarly adapted for this purpose.

In the light of after events, he chose very wisely. The *Endeavour*, on one occasion, 'took the ground' most forcibly, but was 'safely and conveniently laid on shore' shortly afterwards, and patched up sufficiently to let her reach port. She was well built and a good sea-boat, although her small size and coarse lines (she was only 106 ft. long overall, 30 ft. beam, 13½ ft. draught, and very bluff in the bows) made her a slow sailer – this being aggravated, on a long voyage, by the fact that she was not copper-bottomed, but sheathed with wood. While fitting-out, she was slightly modified to accommodate a larger crew than usual. Although officially referred to as a 'bark', the (five) existing sketches of her show clearly that she was square-rigged on all three masts.

The plan of her voyage was materially affected, on May 20, by the arrival of the *Dolphin*, under Wallis – fresh from a voyage of exploration, in the 'South Seas', little more successful than Byron's. He brought news, however, of a group of islands – part of the Low Archipelago – which he had discovered in about 18° S. He had made a long stay at the largest, 'King George III island' (Tahiti), and his account of its amenities, coupled with its advantageous position (almost in the centre of the area laid down by Maskelyne) at once led the Royal Society to select it for their southern station.

Their letter to the Admiralty, intimating this decision, also stated that:

> Joseph Banks, Esq., Fellow of this Society, a Gentleman of large fortune... being desirous of undertaking the same voyage the Council very earnestly request their Lordships that in regard to Mr. Banks's great personal merit and for the Advancement of useful knowledge, he also, together with his Suite, being seven persons more, that is, eight persons in all, together with their baggage, be received on board of the Ship under Command of Capt. Cook.

How the First Voyage Came About 41

The Admiralty granted this 'earnest request' – in the circumstances, they could hardly have refused it. But Cook, even if gratified by the reference to himself (the first on record) as 'Capt. Cook', must have viewed the arrangement somewhat askance. The *Endeavour* was a very small ship; her complement was already greater than the normal; and to fit in another eight (at least two of whom would expect separate cabins) would not be easy. As matters turned out, however, he hit it off very well indeed with the new shipmates who had been so unexpectedly dumped on him.

Banks – afterwards famous as Sir Joseph Banks, Bart., F.R.S. – was a product of Harrow, Eton, and Christ Church. Twenty-four, unmarried, and with £6,000 a year, he had already perplexed the Oxford dons by spurning the classics in favour of botany and entomology – and after going down (not unnaturally) with no great éclat, had made a voyage to Newfoundland as a naturalist. Possessed of a highly independent mind, he had resolved that his Grand Tour should not be the usual dreary and vicious round of foreign capitals steadfastly trodden by the young bucks of his day. 'Every blockhead,' he wrote, 'does that! My grand tour should be one round the world!' With him he ultimately brought his friend Dr. Solander (a well-known Swedish botanist), an assistant naturalist (Spöring), three artists (Buchan, Parkinson and Reynolds) and four servants, two of whom were negroes – a 'suite' of nine persons in all. And in a very short while he showed that he could pull his weight, and something more, as a man – not as a mere 'Johnny-pay-for-all'.

As has been the irritating custom of all maritime officials, of all nations, ever since Queen Hatshepsut despatched her fleet to Punt about 1500 B.C., the Admiralty furnished Cook with formal and precise 'Instructions'. At the time, and long after, the details of these remained secret – although their general tenor became known as soon as the voyage was over. But neither Admiral Wharton (who edited a verbatim reprint of Cook's *Endeavour* journal) nor Kitson ever saw their full text. The late W. G. Perrin, Librarian of the Admiralty, was the first man to look for them in the place where one would expect to find them – the Admiralty file of Secret Orders and Instructions. He printed the Instructions for all three of Cook's voyages in the third volume of the 'Naval Miscellany' (Navy Records Society, 1928, pp. 343–50).

Although couched in Official English, the Instructions for the *Endeavour*'s commander are surprisingly clear. They are in two parts. The first directs him, in detail, to proceed to 'King George's Island' (Tahiti) in good time for the Transit, and to observe it either from that station or, if necessary, any suitable station lying within Maskelyne's limits. He is then to carry out the additional instructions 'contained in the inclosed Sealed Packet'.

I incline to believe that Cook was directed not to break the seal until he reached Tahiti; but there is no evidence on this point. Here is a short abstract of what the packet contained.

It began by recounting that 'the making discoveries of countries hitherto unknown' would be of considerable advantage both to the dignity and (possibly) the trade of Great Britain. There was 'reason to imagine' that continental land might be found in the South Pacific. After observing the Transit, therefore, he was to proceed as follows:

> You are to proceed to the southward in order to make discovery of the Continent above-mentioned until you arrive in the Latitude of 40°, unless you sooner fall in with it. But not having discoverd it, or any

How the First Voyage Came About

evident signs of it in that Run you are to proceed in search of it to the Westward, between the Latitude before mentioned and the Latitude of 35° until you discover it, or fall in with the Eastern side of the Land discovered by Tasman and now called New Zealand.

If he found 'the continent', he was to explore it as thoroughly as he could, and to obtain specimens of its products, if any. If it were inhabited, he was to cultivate friendly, but cautious, relations with the natives; and, with their consent (*sic*), to take possession of it in the King's name. If there were no inhabitants, he was to take possession by setting up 'Proper Marks and Inscriptions, as first discoverers and possessors':

> But if you should fail of discovering the Continent before-mentiond, you will, upon falling in with New Zealand, carefully observe the latitude and longitude in which that land is situated, and explore as much of the Coast as the Condition of the Bark, the health of her crew, and the State of your Provisions will admit of, having always great attention to reserve as much of the latter as will enable you to reach some known Port where you may procure a sufficiency to carry you to England, either round the Cape of Good Hope, or Cape Horn, as from circumstances you may judge the most eligible way of returning home.

He was also to chart, and take possession of, any previously undiscovered islands he might fall in with . . . 'without suffering yourself, however, to be thereby diverted from the object which you are always to have in view, the discovery of the Southern Continent . . .'.

It is to be noted that throughout the whole text of these instructions there is no mention whatever of Australia – or as it was then called 'New Holland'.

None the less, it was incorrectly contended that they did in effect enjoin Cook to do what he actually did – explore the eastern coast of Australia, and take possession of it for Great Britain. I must point out – what may seem incredible – that the propounder of this theory (the late Sir Joseph Carruthers) had previously read the full text of the Instructions: which most assuredly lend no support whatever to his contention. Cook is told, most plainly, to search for the Southern Continent by striking southwestward from Tahiti and running westward between 35° S. and 40° S. until he either sights new land or New Zealand. In the latter case, he is to explore New Zealand as far as he can – and thereafter his search for the 'continent' is, in any event, terminated, and he is to come home by such route as he may select. I need only point out that for a century and more before Cook's voyage it had been a matter of common knowledge that while New Zealand might possibly form part of the 'Southern Continent' – Tasman had only examined part of its western side – Australia could not possibly do so; for the simple reason that Tasman had sailed round it (at a great distance, admittedly, from land) and had, in so doing, passed beween it and New Zealand.

Cook joined the *Endeavour*, in the Downs, on August 3, 1768, and sailed next day for Plymouth. From here, he sent word to Banks (still in London) that he was ready for sea. By August 20 the naturalists had made their way to Plymouth, and were embarked, with their baggage. And on Thursday, August 25, Cook's journal records:

> ... At 2 p.m. got under Sail and put to Sea, having on board 94 Persons, including Officers, Seamen, Gentlemen, and their Servants; near 18 Month's Provisions, 10 Carriage Guns, 12 Swivels, with good Store of Ammunition and Stores of all kinds.

CHAPTER THREE

The First Voyage

The start of a voyage is a convenient time to take stock of one's surroundings and shipmates – and for the same reason I propose to devote a little space here to various points which will frequently crop up in the course of the *Endeavour*'s voyage.

When he left England Cook was confronted, as all previous explorers had been, with two problems – of vital interest to himself and his men – of which no satisfactory solution had yet been given. These were the finding of longitude and the avoidance of scurvy.

As Solomon acutely remarks, the way of a ship in the sea is highly mysterious. Once out of sight of land, her position can only be determined accurately by astronomical observations – and these, however carefully taken, will only give her latitude and her local time; the time of the meridian she happens to be on. Her longitude can only be found by obtaining the difference between that local time and the time of some standard meridian, such as Greenwich – and in the middle eighteenth century navigators had no means of either finding, or keeping, Greenwich time at sea. It followed that the longitudes of their ships – and, equally, of their discoveries – were largely a matter of estimation; or, in plainer English, of guess-work. Wrecks were appallingly frequent – and discoveries had generally to be re-discovered by protracted search along the parallel of their reported latitude.

By 1768 the famous 'problem of the longitude' had, actually, been solved. John Harrison, the Yorkshire carpenter, had produced a timekeeper whose performance more than complied with the terms of the Act of Parliament (12 Anne, cap. 15) offering a reward of £20,000 for a practicable method of finding longitude. Half the reward had already been paid him, and an account of his timekeeper published. But no seaman could hope, at present, to obtain such a timekeeper for love or money.

However, another method had also just become available – one which Maskelyne had done much to perfect. That was the method of lunar distances. If the moon's motion be known with sufficient accuracy, tables can be drawn up forecasting her position in the heavens for a long time in advance; and also her angular distance, as observed on some standard meridian, from suitable fixed stars. These distances can also be observed, by means of the sextant, on board ship; and the Greenwich time corresponding with such distances can be taken out of the tables. The local time of observing such 'lunar distances' can be obtained by the ordinary observations; and the difference, of course, gives the ship's longitude.

Maskelyne had experimented with this method during his voyage to St. Helena to observe the Transit of 1761; in 1763 he published his 'British Mariners' Guide', giving data from which, after some four hours' calculation, a ship's longitude might be found within about 1°; and in 1767, as Astronomer Royal, he instituted the 'Nautical Almanac' – in which he gave, for the first time in the history of navigation, lunar distances of the sun and seven selected stars, computed for every three hours at Greenwich. Green, Cook's

The First Voyage

astronomical colleague, had studied the new method under Maskelyne at the Observatory, and was probably its most able living exponent. Cook, naturally, was eager to learn it – and throughout the voyage he and Green lost no opportunity of doing what most navigators, a few years earlier, would have stigmatised as impossible – obtaining their ship's longitude, at sea, by direct observation.

In general, their observations were correct within 1°, and often much nearer still. This was a great advance. It meant that Cook could navigate freely on the high seas without the ever-present fear of 'losing the longitude'; he could fix his discoveries accurately, and correct those of bygone navigators; and he could re-visit any spot he had once fixed by a course as direct as the winds would allow, and without the toilsome necessity of running it down along its parallel.

In facing the problem of longitude Cook was dependent, at first, upon Green's advice and tuition. But in dealing with the other bugbear – scurvy – he took his own line, based on his own experience and practised on his own initiative.

Unlike Anson and other contemporary voyagers, who seemed to regard the loss of one-third of their crews by scurvy in the course of a twelve months' voyage as almost inevitable, Cook had served for years as a foc'sle hand. He knew, as few men in independent command did, what the A.B. ate, and how he cooked it; where, and in what conditions, he slept; in what sort of state he habitually kept his clothing and bedding – and much else. Also, Cook had seen at least one severe outbreak of scurvy, in the *Pembroke* (1757); and he had formed his own opinion as to how 'inevitable' scurvy really was.

Consequently, in all matters of personal hygiene and dietary the *Endeavour*'s seamen – intensely conservative, as all seamen are – found themselves being persistently and remorselessly shaken out of their 'old, heavy, dull and shapeless ease'. They had to keep their quarters clean, and their clothing dry. Whenever possible, the former were fumigated, and the latter aired. Fresh meat and vegetables were issued whenever such could be procured – and, at other times, sauerkraut or 'portable soup' accompanied the salt provisions. Whatever was issued, too, had to be eaten. And – a grievance beyond all others – their Captain would delegate no part of his responsibility for their health, either to the ship's surgeon or anyone else; when he gave any order on that subject he saw to it, personally and with emphasis, that the order was exactly obeyed. At first they were by no means grateful – they endured his 'fads' simply because they had at once realised that he was not the man to brook their doing otherwise – but they had good cause to change their minds before they saw England again.

The *Endeavour* slowly zigzagged her way down the Atlantic along the well-worn route to the Horn. She spent some days at Funchal (Madeira) where, as was customary, she embarked a supply of wine (in those days, water could not long be kept fresh on board ship) and accidentally lost a Master's mate, who was drowned while laying out the stream anchor. On Tuesday, October 25, she crossed the Line, and celebrated the occasion with the usual ceremonies. Cook's second-in-command, Lt. Hicks, had received King Neptune's accolade on a previous voyage, and took charge of the arrangements. Cook himself, as Captain of the ship, was exempt; Banks and his party compounded for four days' allowance of wine; but some twenty or thirty underwent the usual ducking, with much horseplay and skylarking.

On November 13 Cook arrived off Rio. Here the *Endeavour*'s build, unlike that of any King's ship, and her lack of the customary figurehead, aroused the (Portuguese) Viceroy's deep and unquenchable suspicion. He opined that she was a smuggler or even a pirate, and behaved accordingly – that is to say, with meticulous official insolence. A guard-boat kept a (nominally) vigilant watch, day and night, to prevent all unauthorised communication between ship and shore; men, and even officers, sent ashore on duty were seized and detained; Cook himself, when calling on the Viceroy, was unable to escape the attentions of an armed guard, who shadowed him everywhere. Nor could any effort on his part dispel the potentate's apprehensions; a succinct explanation of the phenomenon which the *Endeavour* had been sent to observe left his bemused Excellency with a foreboding that the North Star was about to pass through the South Pole. Cook returned on board determined not to land again, but to sail as soon as he had embarked the fresh provisions which he required, and which he could not count on obtaining anywhere between Rio and Tahiti.

His supplies came to hand slowly, and at exorbitant rates. Meanwhile, each day brought some petty squabble, or some rejoinder or surrejoinder – for Cook and the Viceroy had engaged in a 'paper warfare', and were bombarding each other with memorials to while the time away. The *Endeavour*'s longboat went adrift, bearing four pipes of rum – but was recovered, wonderful to relate, with this valuable cargo intact. Finally, Cook embarked his last stock of 'fresh Beef, Greens and Yams', put the final touches to a plan of the harbour made from the mast-head, lost a man overboard while weighing (he shipped a Portuguese in lieu) and shifted berth to the outer roadstead. Here he was detained for three days by contrary winds and a last, fond tiff with the Viceroy touching a parting compliment, in the shape of two round shot across his bows, paid him by the Fort. Appreciating at its exact value a lame explanation that the officer in charge had not received the official permit – sent, but by some strange mischance delayed – without which he could not permit the *Endeavour* to sail, Cook at last got away for Cape Horn on Wednesday, December 7.

In accordance with his instructions, he wasted no time in trying to thread Magellan Strait, but made for that of Le Maire, between Staten I. and Tierra del Fuego. Its passage, owing to strong tides and contrary winds, occupied more than three days. On the 15th the *Endeavour* anchored in Good Success Bay, at the S.E. extreme of the mainland, to take in wood and water. Previously, Banks and some of his party had landed in one of the boats – and late in the evening they returned, bringing specimens of nearly a hundred new plants. Fired by this success, Banks took a larger party – Solander, Buchan, Green, Monkhouse (surgeon), two seamen and Banks' two negro servants – ashore next day for further explorations inland. They were caught in a heavy snowstorm – while to add to their troubles Buchan, who suffered from epilepsy, had a fit. Most of the party managed to reach some sort of shelter, and camped for the night around a hastily built fire – but the blacks (who had charge of the rum) lagged behind, drank themselves into insensibility, and were found in the morning frozen to death.

While the *Endeavour* lay in Good Success Bay, a few of the natives visited her. Cook speaks of them as '... perhaps as Miserable a sett of People as are this day upon Earth'. He may, perhaps, have expected too much – Byron, who visited Magellan Strait in 1764, had been amazed to encounter several men who stood a good eight feet high.

Having prepared for heavy weather and struck his guns down into the hold, Cook stood southward round the Horn. On January 30, he reached his furthest south of the voyage – 60° 04′ S., in approximately 74° W. Thereafter he shaped his course N.W., sailing over the position in which the *Orange Tree* had reported sighting land in 1624, and traversing the N.E. portion of Dalrymple's hypothetical continent. Here, for the first time, he was sailing in unexplored waters. His immediate predecessors, Byron and Wallis (as also Bougainville and Carteret, whose voyages were still in progress when he sailed from England) had kept much closer to the coast of Chile when steering northward after rounding the Horn.

Signs of land – sea-weed and tropical birds – were first seen on March 21, and became more plentiful on the 23rd. Actually, the *Endeavour* was not far from Pitcairn I. (whose discovery Carteret had reported in England three days earlier, on his arrival at Spithead). She passed to the north-eastward of the island without sighting it. Two days later, in a fit of despondency, one of the marines – under suspicion of theft – committed suicide by jumping overboard. On March 31 they were nearly in the latitude of their destination, and course was altered to the westward.

On April 4 they sighted their first atoll, low-lying and inhabited. It was the modern Vahitahi, in the Low Archipelago. Proceeding westward in Wallis's track (the *Endeavour*'s Master, Robert Molineux, had served with Wallis in the *Dolphin*) they sighted and coasted several similar islands. Finally, after a day's delay caused by the wind's failing, they anchored in Matavai Bay, Tahiti, at 7 a.m. on April 13, 1769.

It is worth noting – as Molineux must have noted – that when Wallis anchored here some two years earlier, after a passage about as long as Cook's, he had about a hundred cases of scurvy on board. Cook had *none* – an absolutely unprecedented achievement. With simple pride, he records in his journal the success of his methods – not forgetting to praise, also, '... the Care and Vigilance of Mr. Monkhouse, the Surgeon'. His remarks about the use of *sauerkraut* are typical of the man:

> ... The Sour Kroutt, the Men at first would not eate it, untill I put it into practice – a Method I never once Knew to fail with seamen – and this was to have some of it dressd every day for the Cabbin Table, and permitted all the Officers without exception to make use of it and left it to the option of the Men either to take as much as they pleased or none atall; but this practice was not continued above a week before I found it necessary to put every one on board to an Allowance; for such are the Tempers and disposissions of Seamen in general that whatever you give them out of the Common way altho' it be ever so much for their good it will not go down with them, and you will hear nothing but murmurings gainest the Man that first invented it; but the Moment they see their superiors set a Value upon it, it becomes the finest stuff in the World, and the inventor a damn'd honest fellow.

The natives were friendly, and supplies of all kinds abundant. Cook drew up some excellent rules to govern bartering, and enacted that the ship's marketing, for foodstuffs, should be conducted by one person only. This was Banks, who had quickly made his mark as a liaison-officer.

It was the era of the 'noble savage' – that mythical paragon, beloved of eighteenth-century sentimentalists, whose sayings and doings make such works as Gay's 'Polly' and Bernardin de St. Pierre's 'Paul et Virginie' so unconsciously funny. But while Cook and his companions found much to admire in the Tahitians, they could not shut their eyes to the fact that

The First Voyage

there was one accomplishment in which – even more than in swimming and surf-riding – they were 'Prodigious Expert'; and that was theft. They could, and did, steal anything that was not actually screwed to the deck – for example, they robbed a sentry of his musket, and Cook's stockings were stolen from under his pillow while he was lying down, wide-awake. Even when one of the midshipmen shot, and killed, a thief *in flagrante* they were not deterred for long – although it is fair to say that they seemed to bear no malice. And it must be pointed out that, among themselves, goods were possessed more or less in common: while, like the Spartans, they saw nothing immoral in stealing *per se*. Moreover, the temptation to steal was great – in particular the men (and the women too, more's the pity) would do anything for a scrap of iron.

There were seven weeks to spare before the Transit. Cook's first care was to select a site and build a fort – Fort Venus – from which the long-awaited event could be securely observed even if the natives should turn hostile. This done, the instruments were landed – with the result that one of them, the quadrant, was carried off the same night under the sentry's nose. However, the invaluable Banks and some of his native friends took immediate action, and eventually recovered it, piecemeal but undamaged. Banks, by the way, had lost one of his party – Buchan had succumbed to a second epileptic fit. To avoid any risk of offending local superstitions, he was buried at sea.

Barter, botanising and the study of the native customs and language filled in the time. To minimise the risk of missing the Transit through bad weather, Cook detached two auxiliary observing parties; sending one (under Gore, his second lieutenant) to York Island, and the other, under Hicks, to a point on the eastern coast of Tahiti. The great day – June 3 – was cloudless, and almost unbearably hot. Cook and Green, exposed to a temperature which rose at one time to 119° F., watched the Transit throughout its whole duration – almost six hours. They were using identical telescopes – reflectors made by the celebrated James Short – but they found, to their surprise, that their observed times for the two internal and two external contacts – times which, for the successful application of Halley's method, ought to have been in almost exact agreement – differed quite widely (15–20 seconds). However, they counted themselves fortunate that, after coming so far, and waiting so long, they had at least seen the Transit.

Although Green never knew it, and Cook not till long afterwards, another observer had waited *eight years* in the East to witness that phenomenon – and had missed it after all! He was a Frenchman named Le Gentil, who had sailed for Pondicherry in 1760 to observe the Transit of 1761. By a chapter of accidents, including the outbreak of the Seven Years' war, his arrival was delayed, and he had the mortification of trying in magnificent weather to get what observations of the Transit he could from the heaving deck of his ship. Nothing daunted, he formed the heroic resolve of exiling himself at Pondicherry, and waiting for the 1769 Transit. This he did – and while the weather was perfect for weeks both before and after that event, the actual day was overcast, and he saw nothing. Unable to wait for the Transit of 1874, he returned to France – and found that, during his long absence, his heirs had obtained legal permission to presume his death and divide his property among them.

No life of Cook, so far as I know, devotes so much as a line to the effect of the *Endeavour*'s observations of the 1769 Transit upon the problem which they were designed to solve – the determination of the earth's distance from the sun. As this was the original object of the whole expedition, the omission seems unwarranted – and I propose to rectify it.

The observations secured at the northern stations proved to be no more accordant than those of Cook and Green. This was due to a source of error which could hardly have been foreseen or removed. Owing to irradiation, the disc of Venus was distorted when apparently approaching or breaking contact with the edge of the sun, and seemed to be connected with it by a narrow ligament. In such circumstances, the actual instant of contact could not be observed – and the time of its occurrence was a matter of estimation, varying with each observer. Some of the northern observations, too, seem to have been vitiated by additional errors. Much was expected from those taken at Wardhuus, in Lapland, by a leading German astronomer, one Father Hell. But these were so discordant as to give rise to dark suspicions that he had fallen asleep (the Transit began, at Wardhuus, about 9.30 p.m. and ended about 3.30 a.m. – the sun being visible at midnight) and had missed the end of the Transit altogether!

Before the end of 1771, over *two hundred* independent computations of the sun's distance, based upon the 1769 observations, had been received by the Academy of Paris alone. The results ranged from 87,890,780 miles to 108,984,560 miles – yet nearly all the computers were perfectly confident that their particular value could not, possibly, be far wrong. Encke in 1824, and Stone in 1869, 'cooked' the observations into some sort of agreement – but such proceedings have no fundamental value, and are essentially unscientific. The transits of 1874 and 1882 showed clearly that, even with the help of photography, such phenomena do not afford a sufficiently accurate measure of the sun's distance.

It is worth recording, too, that King George's £4,000

proved a good deal more than enough to pay the whole expenses of the observations. The Royal Society spent part of the surplus, very loyally, on a marble bust of His Majesty; and the balance was used to defray the cost of Maskelyne's experiments at Schiehallion (1774–76) for determining the earth's mass.

I return to Tahiti, and the *Endeavour*. Some of her crew seized the opportunity, when most of the officers were busy watching the Transit, to break into the store-room and steal a quantity of iron nails. Cook discovered the ringleader, and gave him two dozen lashes: apparently the most severe – though by no means the only – punishment of the kind that he awarded during the whole voyage.

The theft was more serious than it seems. The nails were the most effectual currency for buying the native women's favours; and this intercourse meant the rapid and permanent infection of the islanders with venereal disease – with which, in those days as in our own, a considerable percentage of any ship's company was certain to be endowed. It had, too, its repercussions upon such of the *Endeavour*'s men as were not previously infected. The matter had already given Cook great concern – but there was little he, or any captain, could do. As he notes:

> ... [It] gave me no small uneasiness, and [I] did all in my power to prevent its progress, but all I could do was to little purpose, as I was obliged to have the most part of the Ship's Company ashore every day to work upon the Fort, and a Strong Guard every night; and the Women were so very liberal with their favours – or else Nails, Shirts, etc, were temptations that they could not withstand, that this distemper very soon spread it self over the greatest part of the Ship's compney. ...'

The First Voyage

He was of opinion – and it is quite possible – that the disease was already known in Tahiti before he arrived there. He inclined to put the blame on Bougainville's *La Boudeuse* and *L'Étoile*, which had visited Tahiti in the previous year – but on what ground he held Wallis's *Dolphin* blameless in the matter is difficult to see. Making the best of a bad business, we may hold, at least, that Cook did not initiate, and did his limited best to control a chain of events which every decent man must deplore; and that, in the long run, it was inevitable that the Pacific islanders should become acquainted with the blessings of syphilisation. Wherever he goes, drink and disease accompany the white man as closely as his shadow.

So indifferent was the health of the *Endeavour*'s men after three months at Tahiti, that Cook determined to explore to the westward (where, by native accounts, he might expect to fall in with several undiscovered islands) before sailing southward, where bad weather was probable. Announcement of his departure caused two Marines to desert; so Cook seized some of the chiefs as hostages, whereupon the deserters were soon sent on board. At Banks's request, Cook embarked a native, one Tupia, as pilot and interpreter; and on July 13 he sailed from Matavai Bay.

He spent a month exploring the westward islands, which he named the Society Isles because 'they lay contiguous to one another'. As he had previously done at Tahiti, he produced an excellent chart of the group. Then, on August 9, he stood southward in accordance with his sealed orders.

These, it will be remembered, directed him to search for the Southern Continent between the meridians of Tahiti and New Zealand, and in lat 35°–40° S. He reached 40° 22′ S., 145° 30′ W. (slightly eastward of Tahiti) on September 2, without '. . . the least Visible signs of land', but contrary winds compelled him, almost immediately, to steer to the north-westward – and between 150° W. and 170° W. he was on the north side of 35° S., while mid-way between he was slightly north of 30°. Just before reaching 170° W., however (a little more than half-way to New Zealand) he was able to get further south again. He reached 39° S., and kept pretty near it for the rest of his westward run; and he had carved another very considerable slice off Dalrymple's 'Continent' when, on October 7, 1769, land was sighted ahead. It was the North Island of New Zealand, which no white man had seen since Tasman discovered it in 1642.

This seems a suitable place to note that the dates of certain outstanding events in Cook's voyage are rather a stumbling-block to the ordinary reader; and that the 'original documents', at first sight, seem to make confusion worse confounded. Thus in Cook's journal the entries relating to the p.m. of any particular day invariably precede those dealing with the a.m.; moreover, the dates in Banks's journal frequently differ by one day from those in Cook's – and while the dates in Green's astronomical journal sometimes, but not always, agree with Banks, they never agree with Cook.

In any particular case, such as the rediscovery of New Zealand now under discussion, the following points should be noted.

There were three different systems of dating in use in the *Endeavour*. Cook kept his journal, and the ship's log, in Ship Time – now obsolete. In this system, the day begins at noon, not at midnight, and twelve hours *before* the ordinary Civil Day. Thus for Cook October 6 ended at noon, Civil Time, on that day, October 7 immediately beginning. Events which happened in the afternoon and evening of October 6 Civil Time (which Banks used all through his journal) would be noted by

The First Voyage 59

Cook as happening in the p.m. of October 7. After midnight Cook (and, of course, Banks also) would write of them as happening in the a.m. of October 7.

On the other hand Green kept his journal in Astronomical Time – a system discontinued in 1925. Like Cook, he reckons his day from noon to noon – but instead of beginning twelve hours *before* the Civil Day, his day is twelve hours *behind* it; and, consequently, a whole day behind Cook's. He would agree with Banks in the date of any event which happened between noon and midnight: he would be a day behind him if it happened between midnight and the following noon – for which period Banks's date would agree with Cook's. Cook's dates would always be a day ahead of Green's: their journals would only agree in always making the p.m. of any day precede the a.m.

As it happens, we are spared a further complication. Nowadays, Cook would have pushed his dates still further ahead by dropping a day when he crossed the Date-Line – which, in the latitude of New Zealand, coincides with the meridian of 172° W. Actually, he did not do so until he reached Batavia – where he notes in his journal 'Wednesday 10th, according to our reckoning, but by the people here Thursday 11th', and continues his journal with the amended date.

By that journal, the sighting of New Zealand is given as 2 p.m., October 7. By Civil time that would be 2 p.m., October 6. Cook has not dropped a day on crossing the Date Line – and, being in approximately 180° W., he is 12 hours slow on Greenwich time. The corresponding Greenwich time is therefore 2 a.m., October 7. And if New Zealand had then been keeping, as she now does, Zone Time – which, in her case, is 12 hours fast on Greenwich – the corresponding New Zealand time would have been 2 p.m., October 7. This result, agreeing exactly with Cook, seems to indicate that the calculation was a waste of time – but it should be noted that if Cook had logged the sighting as occurring at 2 *a.m.*, October 7, the corresponding New Zealand Time would have been 2 a.m., October *8*. All dates here given have been corrected to agree with the Zone Times now kept in New Zealand and Australia.

Cook now had a long job before him. He had confirmed Tasman's discovery of land – although he was on its eastern side, which Tasman never saw. He had next to determine whether it was, as Tasman (and Dalrymple) thought, a promontory of the Great Southern Continent; and to do this he must follow it southward until it either terminated or spread out east and west, merging into a continental coastline.

He anchored next day in Poverty Bay – so named 'because it afforded us no one thing we wanted' – and endeavoured to get into touch with the natives. The Maoris, however, were a very different race from the mild Tahitians – although Tupia, to the general surprise, found he could understand their language. They appeared aggressive, and several were shot. In one case, Cook (in a ship's boat) tried to intercept a canoe-full of natives coming in from seaward, in order to get information from them; but on a musket being fired over the canoe the natives turned on their pursuers, and Cook was forced to fire into them, killing four – while three jumped overboard and were taken prisoners.

If we except the thief shot at Tahiti, this was the first case of bloodshed in Cook's voyages – but not by any means the last. And it is difficult to hold the scales fairly between those who, like Dalrymple, regarded such killings as plain murder, and those who can see no spots on the sun. Cook had a hasty temper – and in this case (as in one or two others) he was plainly in the wrong. He admits, in his journal, that he was not justified in trying to seize the canoe; but he adds, and with reason:

The First Voyage

... had I thought they would have made the Least Resistance I would not have come near them; but as they did, I was not to stand still and suffer either myself or those that were with me to be knocked on the head.

Whenever their duty takes a few men with firearms among many savages who have only clubs and spears, the question of how far might conflicts with right is bound to arise as soon as there is a clash of wills. If you withhold your fire, you will be killed – hand to hand, you have no chance – you must shoot, shoot quickly, and shoot to kill. In such circumstances, men who are normally kindly – and there is ample evidence that Cook was such a man – must sometimes play what seems, to those who come after, a very cruel part. But . . . if they play it often, it is possible that they may cease to realise how cruel it is.

Two days later Cook induced his hostages – who had had the time of their lives on board – to go ashore, and sailed south-westward along the coast. The Maori were occasionally troublesome, and had to be fired over. On October 17 the *Endeavour* was in 40° 34′ S., off a high bluff which Cook named C. Turnagain – for he had found no suitable harbour, and considered that his time would be better spent in examining the coast to the northward. So he went about, and stood north-eastward. Putting in occasionally for wood and water, finding the natives sometimes friendly and sometimes the reverse, he held steadily on his way around this uncharted land. The accuracy of his running survey is nothing less than marvellous, when one considers that it was made in a small and slow-sailing vessel, generally in danger (she touched ground once) and sometimes blown out of sight of land. On Christmas Day he reached the northern extremity of the land, and connected his new coast-line with that discovered by Tasman, whose 'C. Maria van Diemen' and 'Three Kings Island' were easily identified. It is worth noting, by the way, that a French merchant vessel, the *Saint Jean Baptiste*, under De Surville, was in these waters about the same time as the *Endeavour* (she sighted New Zealand on December 12) but the two ships did not meet.

Cook luckily escaped being caught on a lee shore in a furious S.W. gale, which came on just as he was starting to verify Tasman's own explorations by coasting to the south-eastward. Calmer weather followed, and after reaching what Tasman had charted as a great bay in 40° S. Cook put into a sheltered cove (Ship Cove, in Queen Charlotte's Sound) and careened, the ship's bottom being by now very foul. The natives proved, as usual, quarrelsome (although they were willing to sell fish) and Cook obtained evidence – a freshly picked human forearm – to show that, as he had long suspected, they were cannibals.

While waiting for the ship's defects to be made good, Cook climbed a neighbouring hill, and saw enough to satisfy him that Tasman's 'great bay' was actually a strait, and that in all probability the land he had all but circumnavigated was a huge island. Sailing on February 6, he found that, while the tide was running very strongly through the strait, the wind was hardly enough to give steerage-way; and he only saved his ship by anchoring in 75 fathoms. Later, conditions improved, and he was able to complete the passage and shape course for C. Turnagain. He did this to satisfy his officers, some of whom thought that an isthmus might still be found connecting their newly-mapped land with a continent. Their doubts removed, he put about, and began to coast along the land lying to the south-westward of his strait (now Cook Strait).

The coast, behind which a range of snowcapped mountains could be seen, was followed as far as Banks

The First Voyage

peninsula (which Cook, deceived by its configuration, charted as an island) in 44° S. A false alarm of land to the eastward, raised by Gore, was found to be a mare's nest. Then in heavy weather, and losing several spars, Cook fought his way round the southern extreme of the land (reversing his former error, he made Stewart I. a peninsula) and began to coast north-eastward. The South island had shared the fate of the North, and the problem which Tasman had set geographers in 1642 was definitely solved. New Zealand was no part of a Southern Continent.

By March 31, the *Endeavour* was back at the western entrance to Cook Strait, having completely circumnavigated and charted the whole coast-line of New Zealand – some 2,400 miles – in little more than six months. With a slow ship like the *Endeavour*, it would have given no cause for surprise if the chart resulting from such an extensive survey had been grossly imperfect – but, in fact, its general accuracy is amazing. Even to-day, a modern surveyor who could complete a running survey of the same extent and general accuracy in the same time that Cook did would have every reason to feel proud of himself. Hear the testimony of a contemporary French explorer, Crozet, who was in New Zealand waters in 1772:

> I carefully compared the chart I had prepared of that part of the coast of New Zealand along which we had coasted, with that prepared by Captain Cook and his officers. I found it of an exactitude and of a thoroughness of detail which astonished me beyond all powers of expressions and I doubt much whether our own coasts of France are laid down with greater precision.

Anchoring in Admiralty Bay, a little to the north-westward of his previous haven in Queen Charlotte's

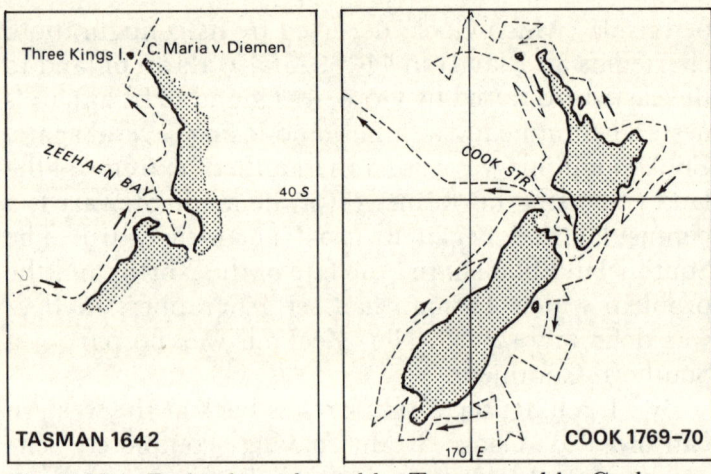

Fig. 2. New Zealand, as charted by Tasman and by Cook.

Sound, Cook began to prepare his ship for the long voyage home. His crew were in good health, and he had still four months' provisions at full rations, which could be eked out by the time-honoured plan of 'Six upon four' – putting the hands on two-thirds allowance, plus any supplies he might be able to obtain here and there before reaching 'some known Port'. But while the *Endeavour* was still perfectly seaworthy, her hull, spars and rigging were plainly showing signs of the hard wear they had undergone; and this was an important factor in determining his homeward route.

His instructions left him entirely free to return 'either round the Cape of Good Hope, or Cape Horn'. The direct route to the former offered nothing in the way of further discoveries. By far the most promising plan would be to stand eastward for the Horn, keeping in as high a latitude as he could. But while this was very tempting – for there was still room left in the South Pacific for a continent (although Cook did not believe that any such existed) – the ship's condition put it out of the question. There was, however, another route which

The First Voyage 65

he could take, and which must inevitably lead to considerable discoveries. And if such existed, it was a moral certainty that Cook – unlike his predecessors – would consider it and, if humanly possible, take it.

At the time of his first voyage Australia was by no means an undiscovered land – as too many people seem to imagine. Between 1606 and 1644 the early Dutch explorers had surveyed and charted, with quite surprising accuracy, three sides of it – the northern coast from C. York westward, the whole extent of the western coast, and the western half of the southern. Moreover, Tasman's 'Van Diemen's Land' (Tasmania) apparently formed the south-eastern point of this enormous territory. These discoveries were no secret in Cook's time – they had become generally known soon after they were made – but two major problems still offered themselves. The eastern coast of New Holland was quite unknown: and the Dutch voyagers had convinced themselves (too easily, as the event showed) that New Guinea and New Holland were connected – that no strait divided them.

It is uncertain what maps of Australia Cook had with him in the *Endeavour*; but it is known that Banks possessed a copy of Dalrymple's privately printed pamphlet *An Account of the Discoveries made in the South Pacific Ocean Previous to 1764*, and that he showed it to his friend and shipmate. It had been given to Banks, shortly before sailing, by Dalrymple himself – a generous act on the part of that disappointed man which could only have been bettered if the presentation had been made to Cook. It contained a chart (on which part of Fig. 3 is based) showing the outline of Australia as then known – and also a piece of recondite information which Dalrymple had learned on the capture of Manila from Spain in 1762. This was, that in 1606 Luis Vaez de Torres, in the course of a most extraordinary voyage (of which very little is known even to-day), had coasted the south shores of New Guinea for some 1,200 miles westward from its eastern extremity. In other words, he had passed *by sea* between New Guinea and New Holland.

Cook was not likely, after sailing over a good deal of Dalrymple's continent, to hold him in great esteem as a geographer. But in this case Dalrymple was not propounding theories, but recording facts; and his facts were cogent. Moreover, in so far as his chart related to Tasman's discoveries, Cook was disposed to put great faith in it, for he had already seen how accurately Tasman had laid down such parts of New Zealand as he had explored. There was little doubt that 'Van Diemen's Land' would be found in or near its charted position; by using is as a starting-point he could find and follow the eastern coast of New Holland; he could coast along this until it either merged with New Guinea or turned westward to form the south side of the strait which Torres was said to have traversed; and thence he could make his way either round New Guinea or through Torres's strait (if it existed) to Batavia or some other port in the Dutch East Indies. If through contrary winds, or for any other reason, he could not coast New Holland, he could still explore to the N.E. in search of the lands supposed to have been discovered – roughly N. of New Zealand and E. of Torres Strait – by Quiros (1606). And so it was decided.

Cook sailed from New Zealand, homeward bound but still 'on discovery', on Sunday, April 1, 1770. He ran westward, hoping to 'fall in with Van Diemen's Land as near as possible at the place where Tasman left it' (i.e. in about 41° S.). But a southerly gale on the 18th forced him northward, and he was in 38° S. when land was sighted on April 20 at 6 a.m. The point first seen, which was named 'Point Hicks' after the First Lieutenant, is a little to the northward of Bass Strait – too far for this to be made out. In consequence Cook, who felt

The First Voyage

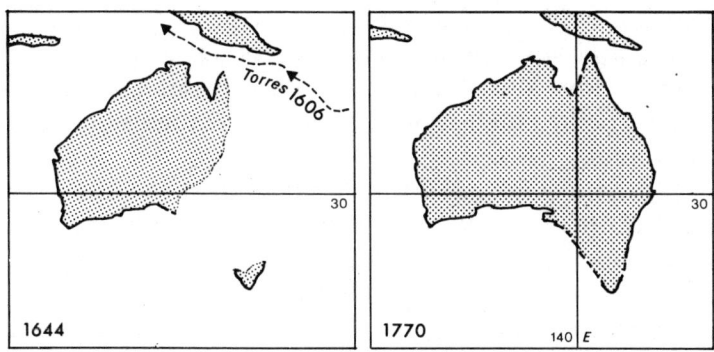

Fig. 3. The outline of Australia, as known before and after Cook's first voyage.

unable to spare the time for a detour southward, remained uncertain whether Van Diemen's Land was part of New Holland, and connected the two, on his chart, by a dotted line. The matter, as it happened, was not cleared up until 1798.

The *Endeavour* coasted northward. For some days, a heavy swell combined with the barren appearance of the shore to deter Cook from landing; but on the 28th he opened a bay which seemed to offer good anchorage. After sending the Master ahead in the pinnace to sound, he stood into it and anchored. Natives were seen, who at first took little or no notice of the ship; but after Cook and a party had landed two of them, armed with spears and throwing-sticks, attempted to scare off the invaders. Charges of small shot induced these defenders of their country to retire.

A week was spent here, water and a plentiful supply of fish (sting-ray) being obtained, while Banks and Solander filled nearly two hundred quires with botanical specimens. The bay was at first named 'Sting ray's harbour', but before England was reached this had been altered to 'Botany Bay'. Cook thought highly – too highly – of its natural advantages. He considered that it would make a very suitable place for a settlement, and his opinion was largely responsible, not many years later, for bringing that result about: the settlers being chiefly recruited (or, rather, conscripted) from among the criminal classes.

For a fortnight Cook continued to make his way northward along the coast, threading his way among islets and shoals with the lead always going. He was in search of a place to heave the ship down and scrape her bottom; but none had yet offered when, on the night of June 11, the *Endeavour* had the narrowest possible escape of being totally wrecked. It was a moonlight night, with a fair breeze – and although Cook had prepared to anchor in about 8 fathoms at 9 p.m., the depths began to increase again, and as he was soon getting 20 fathoms and upwards consistently he concluded that, in the circumstances, he was justified in standing on through the night. He had left the deck when, just before 11 p.m. and immediately after a sounding of 17 fathoms, the ship struck on the edge of a coral reef, and remained fast.

Cook, who was on deck in his drawers a few seconds after the impact, took all seamanlike steps to get his ship afloat again, but for a long while – long, that is, to men whose very lives were bound up with their ship's safety – these were unsuccessful. Ballast, decayed stores and six of the brass 4-pounder guns were jettisoned (attempts were made, unsuccessfully, in 1886 to recover the last-named as souvenirs) and anchors laid out; but the unlucky *Endeavour* had grounded at high-water – and, still more unluckily, at the 'higher high-water'. On this coast, it is only every *alternate* tide that rises to the full height; and, consequently, although the ship was not making much water, and had been much lightened, no efforts could haul her off when the tide had made again – while, as it once more fell, the leak increased considerably as the ship heeled over.

The First Voyage

Back came the tide, rising inch by inch, hour by hour; and as the *Endeavour* righted again she enlarged the leak until it took all available pumps to keep it under. What would happen if they hauled off, no one knew, though all could guess; but it was no time for half-measures. Here was high-water; the ship was all but afloat; and off she must come, or else stay there until the first gale broke her up. And off she came.

For a long time, while Cook was saving what anchors he could, the leak gained on the pumps; and a mistake in sounding the well left all hands, for some time, under the impression that the end was a matter of minutes. The discovery of the mistake put new life into the weary crew; the pumps gained on the leak; and, as soon as it was light enough, Cook cut his remaining cables and edged in for the shore. At the same time, he 'fothered' the leak, hauling a sail (sewn with oakum and wool) over the place where it was surmised to be – the eighteenth-century equivalent of placing a collision-mat. Soon afterwards, the leak could be kept under with a single pump.

The next step was to beach the ship – and a suitable place was found at the mouth of a small river (now the Endeavour river) in 15° 30′ S. It was discovered that the rocks had punched several holes, low down on the starboard side of the bow, as cleanly as if done with tools. Luckily, one hole was plugged by a large piece of rock still sticking in it. A good deal of minor damage had also been done elsewhere; but the ship's carpenters – and, for that matter, the whole ship's company – worked like demons, and in a month the ship was fit to proceed. But it was plain that the days of discovery were over – the most they could hope was that she would carry them, if not too hard-pressed, to some port where she could be thoroughly overhauled.

Meanwhile, Banks and his party had not been idle.

They had acquired a few more plants, and had also studied the local fauna, including an animal which Cook describes as:

> ... of a light mouse colour, and the full size of a Grey Hound, and shaped in every respect like one, with a long tail, which it carried like a Grey Hound; in short, I should have taken it for a wild dog but for its walking or running, in which it jumped like a Hare or Deer.

He might even better have compared its gait to a squirrel's. This was the Great Kangaroo, hitherto unknown to naturalists – although Pelsart, in 1629, had seen some (of a smaller species) on islands off the west coast. Cook himself found time aided by the 'Young Gentlemen' (midshipmen) to survey the harbour at the river entrance; and he and Green, using the mean of two emersions of Jupiter's first satellite, determined the longitude of their encampment (now Cooktown) as 145° 12′ E. – it is actually 145° 15′ E. The natives gave little trouble.

Cook had had enough of coastal navigation. He sailed on August 6, 1770, and slowly threaded his way, conning his ship from the masthead with a boat ahead sounding, through the apparently interminable reefs towards the open sea. As he gradually discovered, he was inside that wonder of the world – the Great Barrier Reef. In the afternoon of the 14th he found a channel (Cook's Passage) through the Barrier, and soon had no bottom with 100 fathoms, while a big swell was rolling in from S.E. He remarks:

> By this I was well assured we were got with out all the Shoals, which gave us no small joy, after having been intangled among Islands and Shoals, more or less,

ever since the 26th of May, in which time we have sail'd above 360 Leagues by the Lead without ever having a Leadsman out of the Cheans, when the ship was under way; a circumstance that I dare say never hapned to any ship before. . . .

But, glad as he was to be outside the Barrier Reef, he was still happier, three days later, to get inside it again. At dawn on the 17th, in a flat calm and a heavy swell, he found the *Endeavour* being set bodily down on to the reef. A sounding of 120 fathoms, no bottom, showed that the reef rose steeply from a great depth, so that he could not save his ship by anchoring – and all that he could effect with his boats ahead towing, and the ship's sweeps manned, seemed to do little more than delay the inevitable disaster. It is interesting – for it is typical of the men who served with Cook – to note that at this moment, with death staring them in the face, Green and two of the officers were engaged in taking a lunar on the poop. Green remarks:

> These observations were very good, the limbs of the sun and moon very distinct, and a good horizon. We were about 100 yards from the reef, where we expected the ship to strike every minute, it being calm, no soundings, and the swell heaving us right on.

As his only chance, Cook made for a small opening which, in the nick of time, showed in the reef. He could not push his ship into it, for a strong ebb-tide was gushing out – but by keeping in this stream he managed to put a quarter of a mile between himself and danger. At the turn of the tide, he got safely within the reef through a second opening, and anchored.

Once more he began 'threading the needle' northward through a maze of shoals. By the 22nd, the land abreast of them was no longer mainland, but islands, between which were stretches of what appeared to be open sea. It seemed likely that, in this instance, Dalrymple was right – that Torres had sailed between Australia and New Guinea, and that the *Endeavour* could follow. Accordingly, Cook landed for the last time and took formal possession of the whole coastline down to 38°, under the name of 'New Wales' (afterwards 'New South Wales'). And then, for the first time since 1606, a ship passed through Torres Strait – to be next followed, twenty years later, by a heavily-laden open boat, carrying Bligh of the *Bounty* and his seventeen companions in the longest and most wonderful boat-voyage on record.

The coast of New Guinea is not exactly a yachtsman's paradise, but to a navigator fresh from the east coast of Australia its dangers were of little account, and Cook would willingly have examined it but for the fact that the Dutch had already done a good deal in this direction. So he shaped course for Batavia, only calling at Savu for supplies. On October 11 (by the local date) he anchored in Batavia harbour, informed the officials (in sole answer to an elaborate questionnaire) that he came 'from Europe', and obtained permission to have the *Endeavour* refitted in the dockyard.

On the 25th he forwarded a copy of his journal and charts to the Admiralty in the Dutch East Indiaman *Kronenberg*, together with a letter giving a short account of his proceedings. In the course of this, he remarks: '. . . I have the satisfaction to say that I have not lost one man by Sickness during the whole Voyage.' By 'Sickness', he implies scurvy; he had lost one through consumption (also one by alcoholic poisoning, two by frostbite and exposure, and three by drowning). No one, before him, had dreamt that such a marvellous bill of health could be shown at the end of a two and a half years' voyage – yet before this ended the *Endeavour*'s death-roll was, after all, to be a terribly heavy one.

The work of refitting was slow, and the Dutch authorities insisted that their workmen alone should perform it. Cook's men were idle; and dysentery was rife in Batavia. When the *Endeavour* got away on December 27, seven more of her ship's company were dead, and some forty sick. Before Cook reached the Cape he had recorded thirty deaths since the ship's arrival at Batavia. Green, the astronomer, was gone; Molineux, the Master; Parkinson and Reynolds, the two remaining artists; Tupia and his boy attendant; and many others. Banks had been desperately ill, as had Solander, but both had recovered. It was a tragic ending to one of the greatest voyages ever made.

Reaching the Cape on March 15, Cook landed his sick, to the number of twenty-eight – of whom three died. Hearing that war between Britain and Spain was imminent (this proved a canard), he hastened his departure, and beat up the Atlantic as fast as his sorely tried spars and rigging would let him. Losing his First Lieutenant, Hicks (who had long been in consumption and had also picked up fever at Batavia) on May 25, he sighted Land's End on July 10, and the Lizard next day. On Friday, July 12, 1771, the *Endeavour* anchored in the Downs, and soon afterwards Cook landed 'in order to repair to London'. He had come home, bringing his sheaves with him.

CHAPTER FOUR

The Second Voyage

Cook was not to be at home for long. No sooner had he passed his accounts for the first voyage than he found himself busily employed in preparing for a second. Actually, he was in England for a year and a day, sailing again from Plymouth on July 13, 1772.

That this should happen was, in the circumstances, almost inevitable. At a time when exploration in distant seas was almost a political necessity, the Admiralty had been fortunate enough to find a man who had shown that he stood head and shoulders above all explorers of the past – a man who did what he was sent out to do (and very much more), who charted his discoveries with amazing care, who fired his officers and men with his own spirit of determination, and who had shown that scurvy could be conquered. All this, Their Lordships could and did gather from the dry, unemotional pages of the journal which lay before them. Yet in his covering letter (from Batavia) which accompanied the journal Cook had written of his doings in an almost deprecating style:

> Altho' the discovereys made in this Voyage are not great, yet I flatter my self they are such as may Merit the Attention of their Lordships; and altho' I have failed in discovering the so much talked of Southern Continent (which perhaps do not exist), and which I

The Second Voyage

my self had much at heart, yet I am confident that no part of the Failure of such discovery can be laid to my Charge ... Had we been so fortunate not to have run a shore much more would have been done in the latter part of the Voyage than what was; but as it is, I presume this Voyage will be found as Compleat as any before made to the So. Seas, on the same account.

By September, 1771, the Admiralty had decided to send Cook out again for the express purpose of finding, or finally disproving, the 'so much talked-of Southern Continent'. In so deciding, they were probably influenced, to some extent, by hearing that a French expedition, under Kerguelen-Tremarec, had sailed from Lorient (May, 1771) to seek the Southern Continent in the S. Indian Ocean – but little inducement was necessary. They had discovered a very great explorer – and while there was so much for him to do he should not lack employment.

Dalrymple and some of his followers had contended, after the *Endeavour*'s return, that Cook had not found the Southern Continent merely because he had not persevered in his search for it. If he had gone further south, they argued, he must have found it – and any modern chart of the Antarctic continent would seem, at first sight, to justify this view. But it must again be pointed out that Dalrymple's Southern Continent was very different from the real one – as conceived by him it was a vast, temperate, fertile expanse affording sustenance to 'probably more than 50 millions' of inhabitants.

Cook had shown that there was no room for a continent, in the western half of the S. Pacific, extending further northward than about 35° S. In the two other great southern oceans, this limit lay still further Polewards. In the S. Indian Ocean, Tasman had sailed south in 1642 from Mauritius to about 40° S., and thence eastward in 44°–49° S., without sighting any land until he reached Tasmania. And in 1739–40, J. B. C. Bouvet de Lozier had traversed the eastern half of the S. Atlantic in about 50° S. with similar ill-success. Bouvet had, however, sighted – in foggy weather – a snow-covered promontory which he named 'Cape Circumcision'. By his account, it was in latitude 54° S. and round about longitude 11° E. Although neither temperate nor fertile, this might conceivably be a point on the long-sought continent – while considerable interest attached to an island in 55° S., and far to the eastward of Cape Horn, which the Spanish ship *Leon* had reported in 1756.

If Dalrymple had been able to consult Cook's journal he would have found, in its concluding pages, a concise plan for settling the question – so far as it related to a *temperate* Southern Continent – once and for all. The Admiralty had already read this, and acted upon the suggestion – which was as follows:

> ... the most feasible Method of making further discoveries in the South Sea is to enter it by the way of New Zeland ... takeing care to be ready to leave that place by the latter end of September, or beginning of October at farthest, when you would have the whole summer before you, and ... might, with the prevailing Westerly winds, run to the Eastward in as high a Latitude as you please, and if you met with no lands would have time enough to get round Cape Horne before the Summer was too far spent; ... thus the discoveries in the South Sea would be compleat.

In the Secret Instructions for the new voyage (which, there is little or no doubt, were largely compiled by Cook himself for Their Lordships' approval) this plan is

The Second Voyage

expanded into a complete circumnavigation of the world in high southern latitudes.

Cook was to touch, first of all, at Madeira and the Cape for supplies. He was then to search for Bouvet's 'Cape Circumcision' and, if possible, determine whether it was part of a continent. If so, he was to explore this as far as he could. If Bouvet's discovery proved to be an island, or if he could not find it, he was to stand as far south as practicable and then proceed eastward – always keeping as far south as circumstances permitted, and examining any land, whether continental or otherwise, that he might discover. Whenever the approach of winter made it unsafe to remain in the far south, he was to return northward to some known place where he could rest and refit – 'taking care to return to the Southward as soon as the season will admit of it'. When, after completing his circumnavigation, he had again reached Cape Circumcision, or its vicinity, he was to make his way to the Cape and so back to England.

For this service, he was to have two new ships. The dangers to which the solitary *Endeavour* had been so frequently exposed in parts of the world where no rescue could be looked for had indicated clearly that there was unjustifiable risk in putting all the eggs in one basket. Indeed, the despatch of the *Endeavour* unsupported had been quite contrary to the usual Admiralty practice regarding exploring expeditions. This practice was now resumed; although, in the event, it made little difference. Two ships were purchased (both built, like the *Endeavour*, by Fishburn of Whitby): the *Resolution* (ex-*Drake*) of 462 tons, and the *Adventure* (ex-*Raleigh*) of 336. The *Endeavour*, it may be noted, was sold out of the Navy in 1774 and re-employed as a collier. Her end is uncertain, but she is believed to have spent her last years at Newport, Rhode I. (U.S.A.), where she ultimately fell to pieces. She is one of a little fleet – the *Golden Hind*, the *Mayflower* and the two *Victorys* (Magellan's and Nelson's) are others – whose names will be remembered so long as men go down to the sea.

Soon after his return, Cook had received his commission as Commander and an appointment to the *Scorpion*, then fitting-out. This was to keep him on the employed list – he never actually joined her, being busily engaged otherwise. He now hoisted his pennant in the *Resolution*. As his second in command he had Tobias Furneaux, who had sailed with Wallis and was now appointed Commander of the *Adventure*. Cook had many of the old 'Endeavours' – commissioned, warrant, and petty officers – with him in the *Resolution*; and he looked forward with pleasure to having Banks's company also. But here difficulties arose.

Banks was as keen to go as Cook was to have him. But Banks, for all his likeable qualities as a shipmate, was a man who combined with a large income a taste for doing things on the grand scale. His 'suite' had been much cramped for room on board the *Endeavour*; although, in common fairness, it must be said that Banks only objected to over-crowding in so far as it affected the party's scientific work, and was not at all careful of his personal comfort. For the new voyage, he designed to bring with him an even larger party, sixteen in all; Solander, Zoffany the painter, Dr. Lind of Edinburgh, and thirteen others, including draughtsmen, servants, and two French-horn players! He objected to the *Resolution* as far too small – it does not seem to have struck him that his own party might be too large – and suggested that the Admiralty should charter an East-Indiaman instead. On this point Cook stood firm, and the Navy Board backed him; but they did their best to meet Banks's cavils by raising the *Resolution*'s upper-works and waist, and

The Second Voyage

building a separate cabin for Cook on top of the poop.

Cook's patron, Palliser, was now Comptroller of the Navy – i.e., head of the Navy Board – and both he and Cook strongly opposed the alterations; not because they wished to cross Banks, but because they considered that the *Resolution*, if given so much extra top-hamper, would no longer be seaworthy. So she proved. While Cook was absent on three weeks' leave, visiting his parents (this is the only occasion on which he is known to have been inside the Ayton cottage – now in Australia), his First Lieutenant, Cooper, sailed with the *Resolution* from Long Reach for the Downs; but after four days' tacking, he anchored at the Nore, and reported that the ship was very crank. In spite of her ballast, she 'lay down' to a breeze in a way which showed her to be top-heavy. One is reminded of that expensive fiasco, the Royal yacht *Victoria and Albert* (as originally designed) which terminated Sir William White's career as Chief Constructor of the Navy.

Cook was still ready to make the best of a bad job by cutting down his new ship's masts, while retaining the new upper-works (except the 'round-house' on the poop) – but the Navy Board had other views. They ordered that the *Resolution* should return to Sheerness and be restored to her original state. Banks – who had spent some £5,000 in equipment – protested in vain. On May 24, 1772, he and Solander inspected the ship; and on his return to London he wrote to the Admiralty, informing Their Lordships that he did not intend to take part in the expedition, and that 'the ship was neither roomy nor convenient enough for my purpose, nor no ways proper for the voyage'. Instead, he visited Iceland with Lind and Solander.

On the main point – the fitness of the *Resolution* for an Antarctic voyage – Cook and the Navy Board were quite right, and Banks entirely wrong. But I question whether, if he could have overcome his stubbornness so far as to embark, he and all his impedimenta could possibly have given so much annoyance to Cook as the naturalist who, at short notice, was 'pitched upon' (the expression is Cook's) to take his place. This was one John Reinold Forster: a German of Scottish descent, a competent naturalist and a most uncongenial shipmate. He and his son, who accompanied him as his secretary and assistant, were both unused and unsuited to ship life. By their own accounts, they seem to have suffered also from what it is the fashion to call an inferiority complex; at any rate, they succeeded only too well in making laughing-stocks of themselves by eternally standing upon their dignity. Add to this that they were chronic grumblers and pessimists, and it will be understood that Cook must often have wished he could maroon his naturalists – a feat, by the way, actually performed by Lt. Charles Wilkes, U.S.N., one of his successors in the Antarctic. In addition to the Forsters, an artist – William Hodges – was embarked in the *Resolution*.

Poor Charles Green had proved his worth in the *Endeavour*'s voyage and in consequence an astronomer was appointed to each ship – William Wales to the *Resolution* and William Bayly to the *Adventure*. Each brought with him, on loan from the Board of Longitude, two timekeepers – the first occasion on which such instruments had ever been embarked for actual use (not merely for test) in an extended ocean-voyage. The *Adventure*'s pair were both made by John Arnold, who was then just beginning his career as a chronometer-maker; the *Resolution* had one by Arnold and one designed by the famous John Harrison.

Their performance during the voyage may as well be described here. The three Arnolds went very badly. Of the *Adventure*'s, one stopped for good before she had got as far as the Cape. The other was stopped, accidentally,

The Second Voyage

while she was there – and although it continued to go after being re-started, its fluctuations of rate were enormous. Cook's Arnold went, badly, for about eleven months – then its winding gear jammed, and it was put aside for the rest of the voyage.

The case was very different, however, with the fourth timekeeper. Unlike the Arnolds, it was in no way experimental, but represented the outcome of many years' labour and thought – for it was an exact duplicate (one of the only two ever made) of the famous timekeeper with which, a few years earlier, John Harrison had won the Government reward of £20,000. It had been constructed by Larcum Kendall, under Harrison's tuition – but Kendall could no more have designed it than he could have designed the *Resolution* herself. In appearance, it resembled a very large silver watch with an elaborately decorated dial and a centre seconds hand. Internally, it was very complicated – far more so than the modern chronometer, for it really consisted of a small and simple watch (compensated for temperature) which would go for 10 seconds, plus another more complicated watch which re-wound the first eight times a minute. Reposing on a cushion in a box with three locks, it ticked away peacefully for nearly three years through alternations of tropical heat and extreme cold, flat calms and furious gales – and its performance would have reflected great credit on the best modern chronometer ever made. By the end of the voyage, we find Cook writing of it as '... our never-failing guide the Watch ...'; and although he and Wales missed no opportunity of getting lunars, it was not long before they came to regard them as, at best, an auxiliary to the Harrison timekeeper. For the first time on record, all through the course of a long voyage a ship could find her longitude within 10' or so, at the cost of only a few minutes' calculation, whenever she could get the ordinary daily observations. It was the real death-knell of the old rule-of-thumb methods, and the beginning of modern scientific navigation.

By July 12 the *Resolution* and *Adventure*, then at Plymouth, were 'in all respects ready for sea'. Their stores – including two and a half years' provisions, ample supplies of Cook's pet anti-scorbutics, and special supplies of warm clothing for issue in high latitudes – were complete, and the men had been paid up to date: in those days an almost unprecedented indulgence. On the following morning they sailed for Madeira.

Cook, it may be remarked here, had left England with the knowledge that his journal of the *Endeavour*'s voyage would probably be published before his return. He had been too busy, as well as too modest, to prepare it for publication himself – and, in any event, the Admiralty had put all the extant journals (at least, so they fondly imagined) into the hands of Dr. John Hawkesworth, a disciple of Dr. Johnson, who was entrusted with writing an official narrative of the explorations made by Byron, Wallis, Carteret and Cook.

This appeared in 1773 (a surreptitious and anonymous account of the *Endeavour*'s voyage, by the way, had been published in London two years before) and proved very popular. It was a curious production. The account of the *Endeavour*'s doings was put into Cook's mouth, but the views expressed were sometimes taken from the journals of Banks, Solander or Green. In many cases, however, they were Hawkesworth's own – and more often than not, very absurd. The style was such as no naval officer ever thought of using. Take, for example, this sentence describing a boxing-match between Tahitians:

We observed with pleasure, that the conqueror never

exulted over the vanquished, and that the vanquished never repined at the success of the conqueror.

And this definition:

OVER-HAULING, the act of opening and extending the several parts of a *tackle*, or other assemblage of ropes, communicating with blocks, or *dead-eyes*. It is used to remove those blocks to a sufficient distance from each other, that they may again be placed in a state of action, so as to produce the effect required.

The unfortunate editor was soon hotly engaged in controversy – not only (this was inevitable) with Dalrymple, but also with some of the 'unco' guid', who thought that he had described certain native customs and views in a manner which showed undue sympathy with them. In fact, if Hawkesworth's three ponderous volumes had been Burton's 'Arabian Nights' they could scarcely have been worse received by the aggressively pious; and the vexation which Hawkesworth had to endure on this account certainly shortened his life. He died in 1773, not long after the book's appearance.

The *Resolution* and *Adventure* reached the Cape on October 30. Here Cook learned from the Dutch Governor, Baron van Plettenburg, that the French expedition under Kerguelen-Tremarec had discovered, in March, what was believed to be a part of the Southern Continent, lying in approximately 50° S., 90° E.: and also that another French expedition, under Marion and Crozet, had discovered two groups of small islands in much the same latitude, but further westward. Here, too, Forster found a new recruit in the person of Anders Sparrman, a Swedish botanist who had studied under Linnaeus, and was then visiting the Cape. Botany not being Forster's speciality, he induced Cook to embark Sparrman for the voyage, undertaking in return to defray the Swede's messing and salary from his own pocket.

On November 22 they left the Cape, making for the reported position of Cape Circumcision. They soon began to feel a decided drop in temperature, and warm clothing was issued to all hands. On December 10, in 50° 40′ S., 20° E., they saw their first ice – one of the huge tabular bergs so common in the Antarctic, but unknown elsewhere. As it happened, this was a small specimen; but it is safe to say that no one on board either ship had dreamed that bergs of such size existed. Next day more bergs were seen, and soon after they experienced that nightmare of all seamen – a heavy gale combined with a thick fog. Driven off his course, Cook crossed the parallel of Cape Circumcision (54° S.) at a point ten degrees eastward of its reported longitude (11° E.). No land was seen, although every now and then a berg would be taken for it – only to have its true nature revealed as the fog thinned off. A field of heavy pack-ice prevented the ships from running westward along 54° S., and so definitely testing Bouvet's discovery – at the imminent risk of shipwreck: but when Cook had rounded the pack, in 57° S., he was able to steer southwestward until he crossed the meridian of 10° E. Having passed 300 miles to the southward of Bouvet's reported Cape, and having for the moment a visibility of 70 miles (from the masthead) with no land in sight, he felt justified in concluding that, in any event, Cape Circumcision was no part of a continent. Some of his officers, however, still clung to a belief that they might have sighted the Cape during their search and mistaken it, owing to the fog, for an iceberg. Cook took the opposite view. He thought it more likely that Bouvet – who also had very foggy weather – had mistaken a large berg for land. The point was left for further examination at the end of the voyage.

In accordance with his Instructions, Cook next turned eastward and began his second voyage round the world. It was obviously going to be a grim job – at least, so long as he stayed in his present latitudes. On his first circumnavigation, he had generally enjoyed – except when rounding the Horn – good weather conditions; but now he faced an almost perpetual combination of fog, rain or sleet, strong gales, and an ice-studded sea. Moreover, while his ships were splendid craft in their way they were not strong enough to contend with the pack-ice. The risk of collision, bows-on, with a berg during fog was inevitable, and must be accepted as part of the day's work; but the floating pack had to be skirted – to push his ships into it meant their gradual, but certain, destruction. Seventy years were to elapse before Captain James Clark Ross, R.N., with the famous *Erebus* and *Terror* – two immensely strong bomb-ketches – succeeded, for the first time on record, in sailing *through* the Antarctic pack and reaching the water beyond.

The ships groped their way eastward, always hauling further to the south as opportunity offered. In about 40° E. conditions improved, and Cook steered due south – crossing the Antarctic Circle on January 17, 1773, for the first time in the world's history. For the moment, he had open water, with only one berg in sight; but more soon came into view as the ships held on their course, and a vast expanse of solid ice-barrier, stretching east and west as far as the (mast-head) horizon, ultimately blocked all further advance. They were in 67° 15′ S., 39° 35′ E. – and, unknown to them, within 75 miles of the continent they had set out to find. Throughout the voyage, nothing is more remarkable, in the light of after events, than the many occasions when Cook was on the verge of discovering land in the Antarctic – only to be robbed of the discovery, at the last moment, by circumstances entirely beyond his control.

He put about, and stood northward; but, before doing so, he got his boats out and watered the ships by the simple process of hewing blocks from the nearest berg – being well aware that icebergs are composed of fresh-water ice. By the end of January 1773, he had reached 49° S. – midway between the two French discoveries (Kerguelen and the Crozets) of which he had heard at the Cape. Being (like their discoverers) uncertain as to their longitudes, and anxious to get south again as soon as he could, he spent no time in searching for them; but on resuming his course to the south-eastward he passed considerably to the southward of Kerguelen's new land, and thus demonstrated that it was, at least, no part of a continent – a fact which Kerguelen himself ascertained, to his regret, in the following December. Cook also passed, without sighting it, within some twenty miles of Heard island, which was not discovered until 1853.

On February 8, the *Resolution* and *Adventure* parted company in a gale, accompanied as usual by fog. Guns were fired, and flares burned; but when the weather moderated each was alone. Knowing that Furneaux had orders covering such an event, and correctly guessing that he would make for the assigned rendezvous in New Zealand, Cook carried on independently without loss of time. He reached 61° 52′ S., 95° 15′ E., on February 24; and although ice-fields again blocked any further advance southward he managed to keep close to the parallel of 60° S. for some 1,500 miles eastward, until he was in the longitude of Tasmania.

It was now the middle of March. The short Antarctic summer was over, and the *Resolution* headed northward. Cook at first thought of making for Tasmania in order to clear up the question of whether it formed part of Australia, but contrary winds decided him to steer direct for New Zealand. He put into Dusky Bay, near the west point of the South island, for a fortnight to rest his crew (he had one solitary case of scurvy on his hands, after 122 days at sea) and then proceeded to the rendezvous in Queen Charlotte's Sound, where he found the *Adventure* at anchor. She had made a direct passage to the south coast of Tasmania without sighting any land. Furneaux – who, it should be observed, was an excellent officer in his way, but not exactly a keen or determined explorer of uncharted regions – then coasted the eastern shore of Tasmania: but he managed to miss Bass Strait – or, rather, he managed to convince himself that it was not a strait but a deep bay. Proceeding to the rendezvous, which he reached six weeks before Cook, he at once made preparations for wintering.

These Cook promptly countermanded. He was determined to continue 'on discovery' as long as he could – unless compelled to, he would not winter at all – and he ordered Furneaux to get his ship ready for sea 'with all despatch'. Finding, too, that there were several bad cases of scurvy on board the *Adventure* (due to a lax observance of his rules) he took the matter vigorously in hand. Scurvy-grass was gathered, and added to the dietary at breakfast and dinner, with the result that the outbreak was soon over.

The two ships sailed from New Zealand on June 7, steering eastward. During the *Endeavour*'s voyage, Cook had done his best to keep to the parallel of 40° S. during his run from the meridian of Tahiti to New Zealand in search of Dalrymple's continent; but he had only succeeded in part, having been driven northward by bad weather almost immediately after reaching 40° S. He now made amends for this in the most ample manner by keeping between 41° S. and 46° S. until he reached 133° 30′ W. At this point he was practically in the centre of the mythical continent, with no land whatever in sight. He now stood northward of Pitcairn island; but a second outbreak of scurvy on board the *Adventure* decided him to push on to the Low Archipelago and then, if it were not necessary to land the sick immediately, make for Tahiti. Meanwhile, he had every available antiscorbutic which the *Adventure* carried administered with vigour; and in a few days a great improvement was reported. On August 16, at daybreak, the ships were on the south side of Tahiti, close in, and found themselves being set on to the reefs by a strong current. They anchored at once; but while the *Adventure* found holding ground, the *Resolution* was not so fortunate, and bumped two or three times – luckily, without doing any serious damage, although losing two anchors. The ships were hospitably welcomed by the natives, many of whom remembered Cook's former visit; and a week later they went round to the *Endeavour*'s old anchorage in Matavai Bay, and re-occupied the fort on Point Venus. Of this part of the voyage, Cook remarks that it shows 'it is practicable to go on discoveries even in the depth of winter'.

From here they proceeded to the Society Islands and, continuing westward, discovered Hervey I. and rediscovered Tasman's 'Amsterdam' and 'Middleburg' islands. These they named the 'Friendly Is.' – but they are now generally known as the Tonga group. By the middle of October they were in New Zealand waters, standing down the eastern side of the North island en route to Queen Charlotte's Sound; but after a series of violent gales the ships again found themselves separated, and the *Adventure* was seen no more during the voyage. Passing through Cook Strait, the *Resolution* reached her old anchorage in Queen Charlotte's Sound

The Second Voyage

on November 3; but time was too short, with the Antarctic summer fast approaching, to do more than refit as far as possible, overhaul stores (nearly two tons of bread had to be condemned) and collect all available vegetables. On November 25, Cook sailed for the southward, firing guns and keeping a sharp look-out for his missing consort – who, as it happened, was coasting down the eastern side of the North island, and making for the same strait that he was leaving. But the two ships were fated not to sight each other again – and Cook bore away alone.

He first stood south-eastward (he must have passed somewhere near Antipodes I., but did not sight it), and then almost due south. The earliest ice of the new campaign was encountered on December 12 in 62° 10′ S. – while on the 15th fog and pack combined, in 66° S., to make Cook alter his course eastward. But he still kept edging south whenever possible – and, again crossing the Antarctic Circle, he reached 67° 27′ S. on December 22, beating his 'farthest south' of the previous season by a few miles.

But the continued bad weather had exhausted both officers and men – the rigging was so coated with ice that the ship could hardly be worked at all. Against his will, Cook was forced to make a long detour northward, reaching 47° 50′ S. in 123° W. But by January 18 he was again on the Poleward side of 60°, and bound south. On the 20th the *Resolution* was once more among icebergs (one of them standing 200 feet out of water) but as she held on her course southward their number diminished, and the air became a little warmer.

On January 30, 1774, in clear weather, Cook reached 71° 10′ S. (106° 54′ W.), a record which stood for nearly fifty years – until 1823, when in exceptionally favourable ice-conditions James Weddell, with the *Jane* and *Beaufoy* (whose combined tonnage was less than half the

Resolution's), attained 74° 15' S. in the sea which now bears his name. Here are some passages from Cook's journal:

> On the 30th, at four o'clock in the morning, we perceived the clouds, over the horizon to the south, to be of an unusual snow-white brightness, which we knew announced our approach to field ice. Soon after it was seen from the top-masthead, and at eight o'clock we were close to its edge. It extended east and west far beyond the reach of our sight . . .
>
> Ninety-seven ice hills were distinctly seen within the field, besides those on the outside – many of them very large, and looking like a ridge of mountains rising one above another till they were lost in the clouds . . . Such mountains of ice as these, I think, were never seen in the Greenland seas . . .
>
> I will not say that it was impossible anywhere to get farther to the south; but attempting it would have been a dangerous and rash enterprise, and which, I believe, no man in my situation would have thought of . . . As we drew near this ice some penguins were heard but none seen; and but few other birds, or anything that could induce us to think any land was near. And yet I think that there must be some to the south beyond this ice . . .
>
> I, who had ambition not only to go farther than anyone had been before, but as far as it was possible for man to go, was not sorry at meeting with this interruption, as it in some measure relieved us, at least shortened the dangers and hardships inseparable from the navigation of the southern polar regions. Since, therefore, we could not proceed one inch further to the south, no other reason need be assigned for my tacking and standing back to the north.

The Second Voyage

No later explorer has succeeded in re-visiting Cook's 'farthest south'; but it seems probable that his conjecture was correct, and that the ice-barrier he saw and marvelled at was backed by the coast-line of the Antarctic continent.

A few days later, while the *Resolution* was northward bound, Cook's health broke down. He speaks of suffering from a 'billious colick'; but it is easy to see that the incessant strain had taxed even his iron constitution. For several days he was seriously ill – the ship's surgeon (Mr. Patten) tended him night and day. Fresh meat was prescribed, and duly obtained from the only source on board – a dog belonging to Forster. After ten days on the sick list, Cook was himself again – as one of the seamen notes, 'much to the joy of the ship's company'.

Still anxious to find, or disprove, the remnants of Dalrymple's continent, Cook searched for its eastern and northern shores as reported by (or attributed to) Juan Fernandez, Davis, and Quiros. Sailing over the first-named position without seeing any signs of land, he turned westward, and resolved Davis's part of the 'continent' into that tiny island which Roggeveen, in 1722, had christened 'Easter island', and whose giant, brooding statues, gazing eternally seaward, constitute one of the greatest mysteries of the Pacific. He also re-discovered the Marquesas, unvisited since Mendana first sighted them in 1595.

Proceeding still further westward, Cook reached Tahiti again on April 22, 1774, and gave his weary crew some weeks of rest. But he still had Quiros's 'Austrialia del Espiritu Santo' to hunt down – the land, somewhere in latitude 15° S., which that noble-minded but incompetent visionary had occupied for a few weeks in 1606, and which he had (inevitably) described as part of the Great Southern Continent.

Two other things were equally inevitable – that (if it

existed) Cook would find it, and that he would prove it to be an island or a group of islands. Actually, Bougainville had already done both in 1768, while Cook was outward bound in the *Endeavour* – but the great French navigator only suspected what Cook (who knew of Bougainville's work) was now to prove. He identified the actual harbour ('Santa Cruz') which Quiros had used, and the bay ('Bay of St. Philip and St. James') out of which it opened; and he resolved Quiros's 'Land of the Holy Spirit in the South' into a small unhealthy group of islands, inhabited by wretched natives. Receiving superfluous confirmation of his re-discovery by being nearly poisoned, along with his men (Cook could eat anything, but sometimes took unnecessary risks in search of novelty), by the same fish which had so disagreed with Quiros's expedition, Cook named the group the 'New Hebrides' and sailed for Queen Charlotte's Sound, adding New Caledonia to his bag of islands en route.

Arriving at his old anchorage on October 17, 1774, Cook found that a message for Furneaux, which he had buried in a bottle, had been removed, and nothing left in its place – but there were other indications that the *Adventure* had come back there in the interim. This was confirmed by the natives, who said that she had stayed some two or three weeks; and they added a story, which Cook did not credit, that a ship had been wrecked on the north side of Cook Strait, and that all her crew had been killed. Actually, as Cook learned on reaching England, this was a distorted account of a tragedy which had happened in Queen Charlotte's Sound itself. A boat's crew from the *Adventure* had landed for vegetables (December 17, 1773) and had come into collision with a large party of natives. All the boat's crew had been killed, and some of them eaten.

It may be as well to note the *Adventure*'s proceedings

here. She reached Queen Charlotte's Sound on November 30, 1773, and found the bottle-message left by Cook, stating that he had sailed independently. Having refitted, she sailed soon after the massacre – the natives were in too great force for much to be attempted in the way of reprisals. Furneaux crossed both the South Pacific and South Atlantic in comparatively high latitudes (he reached 61° S. off the Horn, passing within 45 miles of the S. Shetlands, and 75 miles of the S. Orkneys without discovering either); but, eschewing any excursions further southward, he searched unsuccessfully for Cape Circumcision, and then turned homeward. The *Adventure* reached Spithead on July 14, 1774, over a year before the *Resolution*. It was a good voyage, but not a great one.

Cook sailed from New Zealand, homeward bound after a final campaign in the south, on November 10, 1774. He had already shown that no temperate southern continent could exist in the South Indian Ocean, and that there was no room for even an island-continent like Australia in all the South Pacific. The South Atlantic remained, as far as he then knew, to be investigated. In it Dalrymple, fighting to the last in defence of his beloved theory, had charted south-eastward of the Falklands a huge gulf, 'The Gulf of St. Sebastian', fringed by off-lying islands, and extending over 10° of latitude (see Fig. 4). His authority for this coastline was, to say the least of it, rather questionable – he had found it in a world-map drawn by Ortelius in 1586, and had accepted it with earnest, if not simple, faith; ostensibly, because its N.W. point agreed roughly, in position, with the island seen by the *Leon* in 1756 – actually, because it fitted in with his own preconceived ideas. Cook had the chart, published in 1769, on board.

He asked nothing better than such a target. He crossed the South Pacific in roughly 55° S. (as Furneaux had done the year before), declining to battle further with ice and fog until he was on the eastern side of the Horn. Coasting Tierra del Fuego, the *Resolution* spent her third Christmas away from home in a sheltered anchorage which was named Christmas Sound, and mitigated the monotony of her usual salt beef and salt pork by a large (and, some cynics might think, appropriate) bag of the local wild Geese. She rounded the Horn on December 29, 1774, and Cook spent a fortnight in surveying its vicinity. Then he shaped course for the 'Gulf of St. Sebastian'.

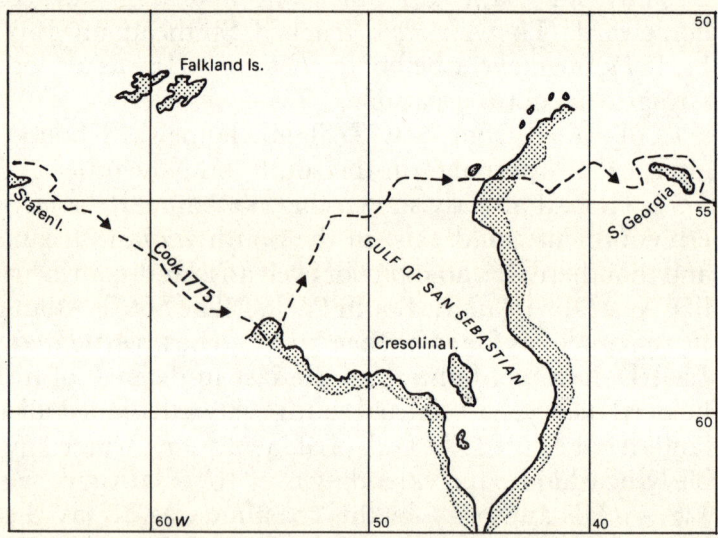

Fig. 4. The 'Gulf of San Sebastian', as charted by Dalrymple (from Ortelius): and Cook's track over its shores.

He knew, by now, more or less what to expect: and he was in no way disappointed – he may even have chuckled – when he sailed through the western promontory of the Gulf, in about $57\frac{1}{2}°$ S., 54° W.; and, a few days later, through its eastern shore when running along the parallel of about $54\frac{1}{2}°$ S. But, while he had wiped the last

The Second Voyage

vestige of Dalrymple's continent from the maps of the world, he put more faith in the island which the *Leon* had reported sighting, and in whose latitude he then was – for the report was only twenty years old, and Dalrymple had certainly not invented it.

On New Year's Day, 1775, land was sighted ahead – the first land, barring the Horn, seen south of 50° S. since the voyage began. It was snow-covered – and for this reason, the Antarctic summer being then at its height, Cook suspected that it was only a berg – but a sounding of 175 fathoms showed that it was really land; lofty, indeed, and extensive, but rugged, glaciated, and utterly barren. Cook coasted its northern side for two days (it proved to be over 100 miles long, by some 30 wide) and made three landings at different points, naming the island 'South Georgia' and taking formal possession.

This was undoubtedly the island which the *Leon* had sailed round in 1756 and named the 'Isla de San Pedro'. It was probably seen, too, by Antonio La Roche (a Londoner, in spite of his name) in 1675; and possibly by Amerigo Vespucci in 1502. But, justly or unjustly, Cook's name for it is that by which it is always known.

Valueless as South Georgia was, its discovery and its appearance gave Cook pause. He could not shut his eyes to the fact that such an island might very easily be mistaken, in foggy weather, for an iceberg – the theory which some of his officers had put forward in 1772 during his fruitless search for Cape Circumcision. He might have missed many such islands in the course of the voyage – but, at all events, he would miss no more if he could help it. Yet the weather was foggy, and his time limited. He worked southward to 60° S., 30° W., but once again he was stopped by the pack, and had to turn eastward.

On January 30 more new land – entirely new land

– was seen, but it was so beset with ice that the ship could not get within many miles of it. It seemed to extend some 150 miles from south to north; the southern portion being possibly a continuous coastline, while the northern was composed of at least three detached islands. He named the southernmost part 'Southern Thule', as being 'the most southern land which has ever yet been discovered', and the whole body of land 'Sandwich Land', after the First Lord of the Admiralty, remarking:

> I concluded that what we had seen . . . was either a group of islands, or else a point of the continent. For I firmly believe that there is a track of land near the pole which is the source of most of the ice that is spread over this vast Southern Ocean.

As we now know, his belief in a Polar continent was perfectly justified. But his 'Sandwich Land' was not part of it. His great successor, the Russian explorer Bellingshausen – who circumnavigated the Antarctic in 1819–21 and filled up all the gaps, along the parallel of 60° S., that Cook had been compelled to leave – showed that Sandwich Land was nothing more than a chain of small islands, whose value for any conceivable purpose was quite negligible. They are, however, unique in being the only land, anywhere on the earth's surface, in their own latitude ($56\frac{1}{2}°$–$59\frac{1}{2}°$ S.).

Leaving his 'Southern Thule' without regret Cook ran eastward in about 58° S. until he was on 'longitude 0' – the meridian of Greenwich. Then he stood to the north-eastward into 54° S., the latitude of Cape Circumcision, and ran along this – firmly determined either to find the Cape or wipe it off the map. A careful search from 6° E. to 22° E. gave entirely negative results; and as Cook, with quiet satisfaction, crossed his out-

The Second Voyage

ward bound track from the Cape in 55° S., 22½° E., and so completed his circuit of the Antarctic, he dismissed Cape Circumcision from his mind as being a convenient, but purely imaginary, starting-point.

Yet the Cape exists to-day – a perfectly real point of land on an actual, but tiny island. Cook was within thirty miles of it when he turned eastward – and Ross, who repeated Cook's search in 1844 but started further west (in about 4° W.), passed eighteen miles north of it without sighting it. In the meanwhile several sealers – Lindsay in 1808, Morrell in 1823, and Norris in 1825 – had fallen in with the island; and the matter was disposed of by Krech in the *Valdivia* (1898) who photographed what is now called 'Bouvet Island' and determined its position as 54° 26′ S., 3° 24′ E. That Bouvet should have seen it at all is one of the most extraordinary 'lucky dips' in the whole history of exploration. Striking southward at a venture, he happened to fall in with a small, glaciated island, not five miles across, which is the most isolated spot in the whole world. It is possible to draw, round Bouvet island, a circle with a radius of 1,000 miles – having an area equal to that of Europe – which contains no other land at all. It is the only spot on the earth's surface possessing this peculiarity.

On February 23, 1775, as already related, Cook 'closed his circuit' and bore up for the Cape – searching, en route, for Denia and Marseveen, two non-existent islands charted by Halley. On March 16 he fell in with two Dutch ships, one of which told him that the *Adventure* had reached the Cape about a year earlier, and had reported the massacre of her boat's crew. He also encountered an English ship making direct for home, and took the opportunity of sending a letter to the Secretary of the Admiralty, reporting his proceedings. She also supplied the *Resolution* with three almost forgotten luxuries – tea, sugar and newspapers. Cape Town was reached on March 22; and there Cook met Crozet, who had been Marion's second in command, and learned of his sub-Antarctic work, and Kerguelen's, at firsthand. Then came the long zigzag up the Atlantic, and on July 30, 1775, the *Resolution* dropped anchor at Spithead. She had come home, from one of the longest and most dangerous voyages ever made, with a total loss of four men in three years – three by accident, and one by a 'complication of disorders' – none from scurvy.

Although overshadowed, both at the time and in retrospect, by the more general interest of the *Endeavour*'s doings, Cook's second voyage is actually the

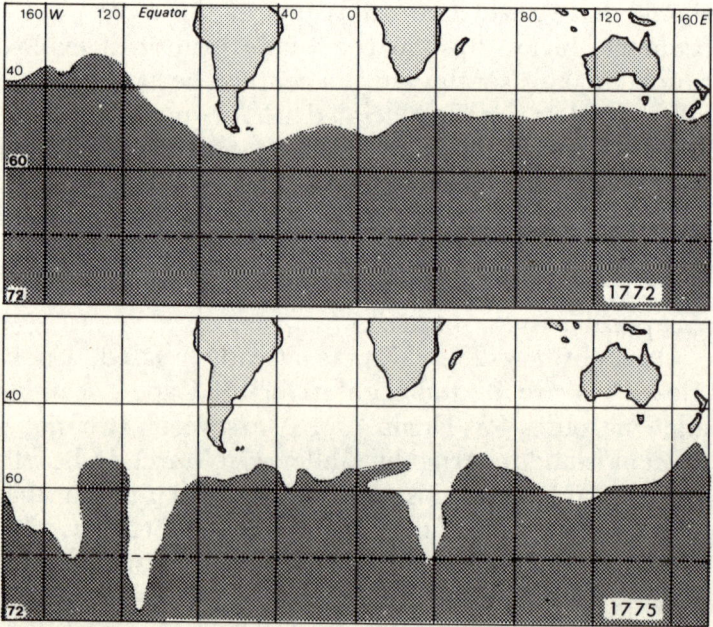

Fig. 5. The 'unknown South', before and after Cook's second voyage.
[The pecked line indicates the Antarctic Circle.]

greatest of the three – and, taking it all round, not far from being the greatest voyage ever made. Bold and correct in conception – although, as we recognise today, it would have been an advantage if the circumpolar course had been set west-about – it was magnificently executed both in outline and detail. The ages-old conception of a temperate southern continent vanished like the dream it was; and, for the first time, the true limits of the *oikoumenê* – the habitable world – were determined. Or almost determined – the north-west coastline of North America was still unknown, and the question of whether it contained some navigable channel leading into Hudson Bay – a North-West Passage, in other words – still unsolved.

CHAPTER FIVE

The Last Voyage

When Cook left England in 1772, he was little known to the general public. But Hawkesworth's book – an immediate success, notwithstanding its many and serious defects – had focused attention on his doings, and he returned to find himself a celebrated man – one, that is, whose name was familiar to many who neither knew nor greatly cared whether New Zealand lay east or west of Australia. Even the war with America, which had broken out while the *Resolution* was on her way home from the Cape, could not crowd her captain entirely out of the news. One paper gravely asserted that he would forthwith be given his flag (he was then a Commander). But his actual reward, if less astonishing, at least included Royal commendation, promotion, and a competence. On August 9 he was presented to King George III and received his commission as post-captain; while three days later the Admiralty appointed him Fourth Captain of Greenwich Hospital, with an official residence and a salary of £230 a year, plus allowances.

Greenwich Hospital – now the Royal Naval College – is a noble building in a splendid situation. A man might well be content to end his days there in peace and dignity, strolling the terraces and watching the ships go by. Yet a letter which Cook wrote to his old master, Walker of Whitby, shows that he felt himself shelved before his time:

(The *Resolution*) is so little injured by the voyage that she will soon be sent out again, but I shall not command her, my fate drives me from one extream to a nother a few Months ago the whole Southern hemisphere was hardly big enough for me and now I am going to be confined within the limits of Greenwich Hospital, which are far too small for an active mind like mine, I must however confess it is a fine retreat, and a pretty income, but whether I can bring my self to like ease and retirement, time will shew.

For a short time he occupied himself in his little house at Mile End (he seems never to have taken up his residence at Greenwich) with preparing his journal of the second voyage for publication. It was originally intended that the official account should be in two volumes – Cook's journal of the voyage and Forster's scientific observations. But Forster would not agree to this. By his account, the First Lord (Sandwich) had promised him, through a third party (the Hon. Daines Barrington) before sailing, that he, and no one else, should write the full history of the voyage – that he should have every penny of the profits – and that he should thereafter be provided with permanent Admiralty employment. Naturally, no one would accept these ridiculous statements – and, as he proved quite intractable, he was ultimately told that Their Lordships forbade him to publish anything on the subject. On the other hand, the Admiralty were aware that the result of commissioning Dr. Hawkesworth to put explorers' journals into literary shape had not been too happy; and it was determined that Cook himself should prepare a full account of the whole voyage (based, of course, on his journal) and that this should be revised – but not altered in any essentials – by the Rev. John Douglas, Canon of Windsor.

Meanwhile, as Cook had told Walker, a new voyage of discovery was being planned. The Admiralty were anxious to set at rest, if possible, the rumours (which had been current ever since Drake's time) that a navigable channel ran from the west coast of North America to Hudson Bay; and, at the same time, to determine whether a north-west passage from Europe to Asia could be accomplished by sailing round the (unknown) northern extremity of the Canadian mainland. With this end in view, it was decided that an expedition should repeat Drake's attempt of 1579 – enter the Pacific, coast the western side of the American continent northward, and endeavour to force a passage eastward into either Hudson Bay or Baffin Bay.

At this time, the northward and westward extent of North America was very little known; and such definite information as was available (which is roughly shown in Fig 6) had given rise to widely divergent opinions. At the south-eastern end of this unknown coastline, exploration had not advanced much beyond Drake's 48° N.; but at the north-western end Russian explorers, voyaging from bases in Kamchatka, had made considerable progress. In 1728 Veit Bering (following the long-forgotten track of Deshnef in 1648) had rounded the eastern extremity of Asia, East Cape (now C. Deshnef); while two years later Gvosdev discovered land opposite East Cape, forming the eastern shore of the strait which now bears Bering's name. In his second voyage (1741), the latter sighted land in about 60° N., 140° W. (Mt. St. Elias) and at many other points during a westward run which took him, ultimately, along the south side of the Aleutian islands. Meanwhile his second in command, Chirikov, had sighted a small extent of coastline a long way south-eastward of Mt. St. Elias, and in about 56° N.

A map drawn by Muller (who took part in Bering's

The Last Voyage

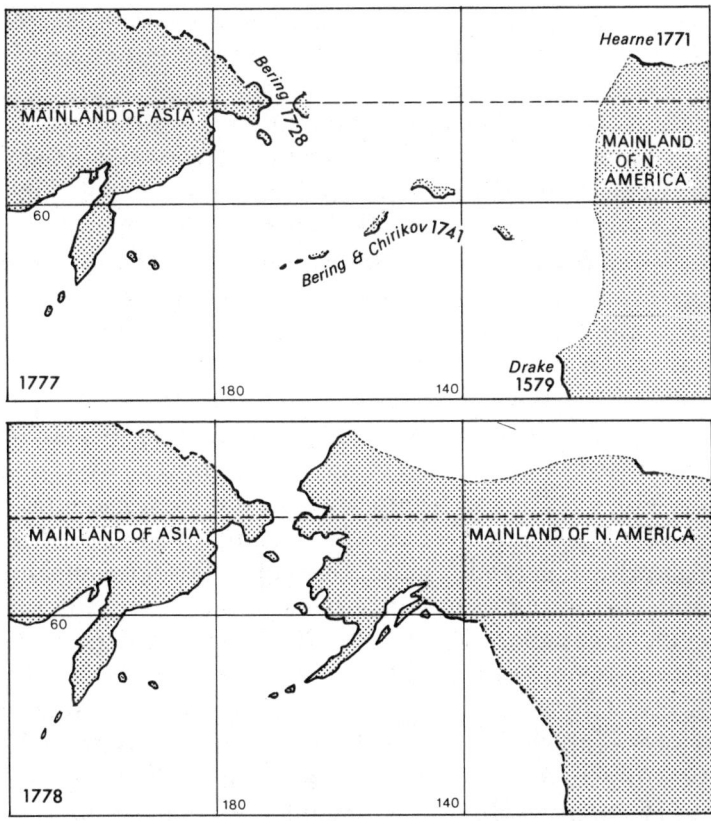

Fig. 6. The N.W. coast of North America, and Bering Strait, as known before and after Cook's explorations in 1778.

second voyage) and published by the St. Petersburg Academy of Sciences in 1754 (revised, 1758) adopted the view (now known to be correct) that all the detached portions of coastline seen by Bering and Chirikov eastward of the meridian of Bering Strait were part of the North American mainland – and therefore continuous with the 'New Albion' which Drake had followed northward to 48° N. On the other hand some geographers, such as Stœhlin and Campbell, considered that there was insufficient evidence to prove that Bering had seen anything more than an extensive archipelago, through which vessels could push far to the northward.

Yet again, geographers of the Dalrymple type, such as J. N. Delisle, plumped whole-heartedly for a channel or channels running from the unknown coast northward of 'New Albion' into Hudson Bay (a view which even Muller did not entirely reject). This they based upon various stories – some wholly apocryphal, some merely distorted – of ships having entered such channels and voyaged far into the interior of the North American continent. They laid stress upon the strait supposed to have been discovered in 47°–48° N. by Juan de Fuca (1593) and still more upon that, in 53° N., along which de Fonte was said to have sailed north-eastward, in 1640, until he met a ship from Boston, New England!

Belief in such a channel – the mythical 'Strait of Anian' – lingered for many years after this date; in fact, until Vancouver's great survey of 1792–94. But the evidence available even in 1776 showed that no such channel could run into Hudson Bay or lie outside the Arctic Circle. Repeated explorations of the western shores of the bay had failed to find any inlet that could possibly be the eastern end of such a channel; and in 1771 Samuel Hearne, travelling northward *overland* to the westward of Hudson Bay, had reached the shores of the Arctic Ocean in 68° N. (72° by his reckoning) – showing that no through channel could exist in a lower latitude. But while such explorations proved that a North-West Passage could never be found in temperate latitudes, they did not forbid the supposition that one might exist further north.

This was the problem, then, which the Admiralty set themselves to solve: a problem second only in importance to that of the Southern Continent. Obviously, the man who had solved the one was the fittest person to grapple with the other – and so it came about. Cook

The Last Voyage

was invited out of his 'fine retreat' to dine with Sandwich (First Lord), Palliser (Controller) and Stephens (Secretary) – ostensibly, to discuss the expedition and advise as to the selection of its leader – and, as had probably been anticipated, he volunteered for the command. It goes without saying that he was appointed – his billet at Greenwich being secured to him on his return.

He was to have the *Resolution* again; but his consort this time was the *Discovery*, a smaller ship (229 tons) than the *Adventure*, but a fine sailer – as Cook soon found, she could claw off a lee-shore much better than his own ship. Her captain was to be Charles Clerke, who had previously served in the *Endeavour* as Master's Mate (afterwards Lieutenant) and in the *Resolution* as Lieutenant. Cook's First Lieutenant was Gore, who had been with him in the *Endeavour*, and his Master was William Bligh, who afterwards rose to fame (of a peculiar kind) through being twice deposed by mutinous subordinates – once when captain of the *Bounty* and again when Governor of New South Wales. Several of Cook's former warrant and petty officers were also serving with him again – and he had an unusual shipmate in the person of Omai, a Tahitian whom Furneaux had brought to England, and who seems, on the whole, to have made a good impression there; although his rather precipitate way with women brought about, at first, one or two embarrassing situations.

Bayly, the *Adventure*'s astronomer, was appointed to the *Discovery*. None was provided for the *Resolution*, as both Cook and his Second Lieutenant, King, were fully qualified for such duty. The Harrison timekeeper, which had performed so wonderfully on the recent voyage, went with Cook, while the *Discovery* had one (K 3) designed and made by Kendall. It was much simpler than the Harrison, but did not go so well. The equipment of the ships was on much the same lines as for the previous voyages, except that each carried the frames of a 20-ton schooner – which could, if required, be erected and used to explore channels too narrow for the ships to enter. An artist (Webber) accompanied the expedition, but no naturalists – Anderson, Cook's surgeon, undertaking this duty. Sufficient annoyance was, none the less, provided by some livestock – which, on board ship, are inevitably and literally a filthy nuisance. It was King George's benevolent intention that these animals (a bull, two cows and their calves, and some sheep) should be put ashore, at such Pacific islands as Cook thought best, for the benefit of the natives.

By the end of June, 1776, the ships were waiting at Plymouth for their final instructions, which were received on July 8. They differed in two respects from those of the first and second voyages; they were only nominally 'secret', and they gave specific dates for the arrival of the ships at various places. Briefly, they were as follows.

After touching at Madeira and the Cape, Cook was to search for the islands discovered by Crozet and Kerguelen, and (if possible) find a good harbour in one of them. But he was not to spend much time in this service, taking care to reach either Tahiti or the Society Is. (where he was to land Omai) in good time to rest his men before proceeding northward. He might, however, touch at New Zealand en route.

He was to leave the Society Is. in February, 1777, or sooner if necessary, and make the 'Coast of New Albion' in about 45° N. He was then to coast northward, without stopping to examine any inlets until he reached latitude 65° N., 'where we could wish you to arrive in the month of June next' (1777). He was then to search for an inlet running towards Hudson Bay or Baffin Bay. If none such could be found, he was to winter in Kam-

The Last Voyage

chatka, or elsewhere at his discretion; and in the following year (1778) he was to go further northward in search of either a North-West Passage into the Atlantic, or a North-East Passage into the North Sea. Finally, he was to come home by whatever route he thought best.

Cook, who had a hand in drafting these instructions, was a very temperate man – otherwise one would be tempted to imagine that they were sketched out at Sandwich's dinner-table. Certainly they breathe a spirit of almost post-prandial optimism. The selection of latitude 65° N. as a starting-point was perfectly justified, in view of Hearne's overland journey – and there was some ground for holding, with Stœhlin, that the American mainland did not extend far westward of 'New Albion'; but the time allowed Cook for reaching the latter presupposed a succession of fair winds – while the remainder of the programme could only have been performed, as scheduled, by aeroplane. Actually, Cook reached 65° N. in August, 1778, instead of June, 1777 – the North-East Passage took Nordenskjöld, a century later, two years to make (1878–79) with the help of steam – and Amundsen, with similar advantages, took twice as long (1903–07) over the North-West.

The *Resolution* left Plymouth on July 11. The *Discovery* was left behind – Clerke had incautiously backed a bill for his brother, and had taken sanctuary from the 'Israelites' in the Rules of the King's Bench (where he contracted consumption). However, he managed to escape to his ship, and joined Cook at the Cape on November 10. Here Cook, as instructed, picked up some more livestock, and his ship began to look like Noah's ark. Incidentally, he had already found that her refit had been far from thorough – her upper-works leaked, while her spars and masts were a constant source of trouble throughout the voyage. Here, too, he may have heard a canard (it was certainly current at the Cape soon afterwards) that a strait had recently been discovered to run from the Pacific (in latitude 47° 45′ N.) to Hudson Bay.

Sailing on November 30 (already three weeks behind schedule) Cook ran eastward along latitude 47° S., and on December 12 sighted the western of the two groups of islands discovered by Marion and Crozet in 1772. These were un-named on the chart given him by Crozet at the Cape in 1775; so he christened them the 'Prince Edward islands' after the Duke of Kent (father of Queen Victoria). The eastern group (the Crozets) was sighted and examined three days later. Cook then bore a little further southward, meeting with very cold and foggy weather, and made the north-west end of Kerguelen on December 24. A reasonably good harbour (Christmas Harbour) was found here, and a stay of three days made; but while a good supply of water was secured, the coarse grass proved hardly worth cutting for the animals, whose feed was already becoming a problem (several died at Kerguelen or soon after). After noting his visit on a bottled parchment left by Kerguelen, Cook made a running survey down the southeastern coast in bad weather, and then bore away for New Zealand.

On February 12 the *Resolution* and *Discovery* reached Cook's old anchorage in Queen Charlotte's Sound. The Maoris imagined, at first, that they had come to avenge the massacre of the *Adventure*'s boat's crew; and, although they were set at ease on this point, they remained rather suspicious. However, two of the natives volunteered to accompany Omai – 'having', one supposes, 'a mind to try their fortune that way' – and, although warned that they would not be able to return, soon made themselves quite at home on

The Last Voyage 109

board. Here, too, both Lt. King and Anderson showed that they possessed Banks's ability to get on friendly terms with the natives; while Anderson, in particular, revealed a remarkable capacity for learning native languages and studying tribal customs.

Sailing on February 25, 1777, for Tahiti, Cook found himself persistently baffled by head-winds. By the beginning of May (he was expected, according to his Instructions, to have *left* Tahiti three months earlier) he was still some 10° to leeward of it, and vigorously seeking fodder for the remaining livestock (some had been left in New Zealand) among some newly discovered islands – now the Cook Is. – southward of Hervey I. He met with little success; and, although Hervey I. itself promised better supplies, no anchorage could be found there. At the same time, however, he obtained a very striking proof – although no further proof was really needed – of the accuracy with which his Harrison timekeeper went. When he discovered Hervey I. in 1773, while sailing westward, its longitude by the timekeeper (based on that of Tahiti) was 158° 54' E. Now, sailing eastward, the same timekeeper gave its longitude (based on that of Queen Charlotte's Sound) as 159° 04' E. – a difference of 10' only (in that latitude, roughly nine nautical miles).

If Cook had had no livestock on board, and had therefore been able to spend long periods at sea without touching for forage, he would have made a long detour to the southward in search of a westerly wind which should take him towards the meridian of Tahiti. But, circumstanced as he was, it was necessary – Instructions or no Instructions – to alter his plans. He could not hope, as matters stood, even to make the coast of New Albion before September; which meant starting to coast northward at a season when, in very similar latitudes on the other side of North

America, he had always been forced, by bad weather, to suspend his surveys until next season. No useful work could be done in such circumstances; he would have to defer his northern explorations until the following spring. Meanwhile, he would perform his minor commissions, land Omai and the livestock, rest his men, and refit his ships.

Accordingly, he bore away for the Friendly Is. (Tonga group), where the ships spent some two months. The natives, many of whom remembered Cook's former visit during his second voyage, lived up to the name he had given the group – but their pilfering was incessant, and even flogging had little or no deterrent effect.

By August 12 the ships were at last off the southeastern end of Tahiti, where they anchored for a few days. Here Cook learned, to his surprise, that some European animals (goats, pigs, dogs, a bull and a ram) had already been landed by two ships which had visited the island twice since he was last there (1774). They proved to be Spaniards, from Lima. He found a cross which they had erected, inscribed 'CHRISTUS VINCIT. CAROLUS III IMPERAT. 1774', and had a supplementary inscription, noting the prior visits made by Wallis and himself, cut on the back, as follows – 'GEORGIUS TERTIUS REX. ANNIS 1767, 1769, 1773, 1774 & 1778'.

On August 23, 1778, he anchored once more in Matavai Bay. Here, to his great relief, he landed the remainder of the animals brought from England. Among these were two saddle-horses, which he and Clerke used to ride daily, a proceeding which never failed to astonish the natives. With Anderson's help, Cook obtained much new information relating to the native customs and rites – in particular they attended, but did not actually witness, a human sacrifice.

Cook decided, with Omai's consent, to land him at

The Last Voyage 111

Huahine, in the Society Is. (where he had some relatives living), and not at Tahiti. Here, accordingly, he was put ashore, with all his European goods and presents, at the end of October and left in the occupation of a house and garden which had been built and laid out for him. While this was being done, there occurred one of the few events in Cook's life which one would like to forget. Bayly's sextant was stolen; and Cook, who was seriously ill with fever at the time, let his anger get the better of him. When the sextant had been recovered, and the thief surrendered, he had the man's head shaved and his ears cut off. He speaks of the culprit, in his journal, at 'a hardened scounderal' – and for such men English law, even in that century, had once sanctioned similar brutal punishments – but the act was unworthy of any civilised man. Later, with returning health, he admitted as much, and expressed sincere regret for what he had done.

After purchasing at Borabora an anchor which Bougainville had left there, the *Resolution* and *Discovery* sailed, on December 8, 1777, to begin their first campaign in the north. They crossed the Line on the 23rd, and two days later fell in with an undiscovered island which afforded them about three hundred good-sized turtle and a plentiful supply of fish. An eclipse of the sun was observed during their stay, but the beginning was obscured by cloud, and could not be timed. Cook named the island 'Christmas Island', and sailed northward again on January 2, 1778.

Another discovery, of much greater value, was awaiting him. On January 18 he notes:

> At day-break saw an island at a great distance bearing NEbE½E, and soon after saw another bearing NbW. Sounded with a line of 150 fathoms, but did not strike ground.

On the following day another island, more distant, came into view in the north-west. In order of sighting the three were Oahu, Kauai and Nihau – all forming part of the Hawaiian group.

Much ink has been spilt over the question of whether Cook was the original discoverer of this group, or whether they were previously known to Europeans. Burney – who was with Cook in this voyage, and who afterwards proved himself the historian *par excellence* of Pacific exploration – identified them in later years (following Humboldt) with a group said to have been discovered, about 1542, by Juan Gaetano; and this has been accepted by many later geographers. On the other hand Dahlgren, in a monograph published at Stockholm in 1916, has shown that neither Gaetano nor any *known* explorer before Cook can claim the discovery. If made (and it is possible that some one of the Spanish treasure-ships may have done this, while there are several native traditions of white men having reached the group before 1778) we must either assume that the discoverer never returned to civilisation, or that he left no precise account of his feat on record. Cook, himself, undoubtedly believed that his discovery was original; and there is no doubt that he was the first man to make details of the group's existence, position and extent generally available. Following what might almost be called his usual custom, he named it the 'Sandwich Islands' – having thus affixed the First Lord's name to a group of islands on either side of the equator, as well as to another island in the New Hebrides (now Efate). Actually, this was a work of supererogation. John Montagu, fourth earl of his name, will always be best remembered as the eponym of the sand'wich.

Cook had no time to explore the rest of the group. He anchored for two days at Kauai, and found the natives

The Last Voyage

friendly, but thievish. One of the boats, sent for water, was mobbed by a crowd anxious to steal every moveable article; and Williamson, the lieutenant in charge, was obliged to shoot (and kill) one man before he could drive them off. This incident, as will be seen later, preyed on his mind – and, there is little doubt, indirectly brought about Cook's own death.

After touching at Nihau, the ships sailed for the North American coast on February 2, and fell in with it (in latitude 44° 33′ N.) on March 7. In accordance with his instructions, Cook began to coast northward in stormy weather, which compelled him to keep well off shore. Owing to this, he passed the reputed position of de Fuca's strait (47°–48° N.) without seeing any signs of it, and concluded that it did not exist. This was an error – the old Greek's name is justly attached, on modern charts, to the wide strait (in latitude 48° 20′ N.) dividing the south end of Vancouver I. from the mainland, and leading to Puget Sound – but not, alas, to the Atlantic.

On March 29 the *Resolution* and *Discovery* anchored in what Cook took to be a small inlet of the mainland. It was actually Nootka Sound, in Vancouver island. They remained here for nearly a month, as the *Resolution*'s masts and rigging were again giving trouble. The mizzen was past saving, and a new mast had to be cut and fitted. The natives, as usual, proved consummate thieves – in addition, they demanded payment for everything, down to wood and water, taken on board the ships.

Cook sailed on April 26, and immediately encountered a violent gale, which blew both ships a long way off-shore. In fact, in the course of a long slant northwestward they only saw the coast at a few points before sighting (on May 4) a snow-covered mountain which Cook identified with Bering's Mt. St. Elias. He was now in about 60° N., 140° W. (roughly 1,000 miles N.W. from his anchorage at Nootka) and, although his survey of the intermediate coast had been very imperfect, he was convinced by now that the American continent extended much further in this direction than he had supposed.

Proceeding westward, Cook was able to follow the coast much more closely than Bering had done, and filled up many gaps in the latter's work. He examined and charted the bay which Bering had roughly indicated westward of Mt. St. Elias, naming it 'Prince William's Sound'. Rounding the Kenai peninsula, he next discovered a larger inlet (now Cook Inlet) running a long way north-eastward. Although sceptical as to its being the long-sought passage, he made his way up it – and also up a long arm opening out of it to the eastward – until the channel had become impracticably narrow and the water almost fresh. Returning to the open sea, the ships made their way round the end of the Alaskan peninsula, and so into Bering Strait. On August 3, Anderson, the *Resolution*'s surgeon, who had been seriously ill for some months, died of consumption. Cook gave his name to the next island met with, '. . . to perpetuate the Memory of the deceased, for whom I had a very great regard'. Such praise from Cook – whose stern sense of duty made him very sparing of it – speaks volumes for the dead surgeon's character and conduct. Given health and further opportunities, he would, I think, have made a great name for himself as a pioneer of scientific ethnology.

On August 9 the ships anchored, on the American side, in the narrowest portion of Bering Strait, where the two continents are less than forty miles apart. Cook named the western point of America (un-named by Gvosdev, its discoverer) 'C. Prince of Wales'. Stœhlin's map, which Cook had previously been dis-

The Last Voyage

posed to accept, was here finally proved to be quite untrustworthy – on the other hand he remarks:

> In justice to Behring's memory, I must say he delineated this coast very well, and fixed the latitude and longitudes of the points better than could be expected from the methods he had to go by.

The season was getting late, and it was hopeless to try for either a north-west or north-east passage home until after the winter. However, Cook determined to explore as far as he could, and pushed northward until stopped by pack-ice in 70° 44' N. Standing east and west, he then charted the coast-line on both sides of the northern approach to Bering Strait; and, after re-passing C. Prince of Wales, examined the large inlet south-eastward of it, which he named Norton Sound. He was back at Unalaska (Aleutian Is.), where he had touched in the beginning of August, on October 2; and here, for the first time, he fell in with some Russian traders who had sent him several letters by native bearers. Unfortunately, no one on board either ship could speak Russian; none of the Russians spoke English; and efforts to find a common tongue were fruitless. However the leader of the Russians – a pilot named Ismailov – proved a very intelligent man and a good cartographer, and Cook was able to get much useful information from him in an intercourse conducted chiefly by signs and figures.

On October 26 the ships sailed for the Hawaiian group, Cook having decided to winter there rather than at Petropavlosk, where his men would perforce be idle for some six months. He made Maui – lying towards the south-western end of the group, and not previously seen – on November 26; and on the 30th the ships came in sight of Hawaii. This being much larger than the remaining islands, Cook spent some seven weeks in charting it, putting in occasionally for supplies. Finally, on January 17, 1779, the ships anchored in Kealakekua Bay (on the western side of the island) to refit.

Here three weeks were spent. The natives proved both friendly and generous – while the personal honours lavished upon Cook himself seemed, at first, both embarrassing and inexplicable. Later, it was found that the natives believed him to be a reincarnation of one Lono, or Orono (a mythical personage, half hero, half god) and regarded him as more than human. The king and the principal chiefs vied with each other in paying him ceremonial attentions amounting almost to adoration – while they strained the resources of the island to provide supplies for the expedition. Nor were the rank and file of the natives behind-hand in doing the same – although they showed themselves as great thieves as any that the ships had encountered elsewhere.

On February 4 the *Resolution* and *Discovery* left Kealakekua Bay to complete their survey of Hawaii. Cook intended, when this was finished, to examine Maui and connect his recent survey with that part of the group which he had examined twelve months earlier. Thereafter, he would stand once more to the northward and, in Hudson's noble phrase 'achieve what he had undertaken, or else give reason wherefore it could not be'. So he planned – while, unknown to him, the last sands of his life were running out. In a fortnight, he would belong to the ages.

CHAPTER SIX

Cook's Death – and After

On February 6, two days after sailing, the ships met with a severe gale; in the course of which, *more suo*, the *Resolution* sprung her top-mast. Cook put back to Kealakekua Bay, where he anchored on the 11th, and at once had the repairs put in hand. The natives, while still friendly, appeared far less cordial, and several 'incidents' occurred; the most serious being the theft of the *Discovery*'s cutter in the night of February 13–14.

Cook determined to land and seize either the king or one of the principal chiefs, as a hostage against the return of the cutter. Accordingly on the morning of Sunday, February 14, he manned and armed boats, and stationed them in a cordon across the bay, to stop all traffic. He despatched King to the observatory (on the other side of the bay) with instructions to quiet the natives in its vicinity; while he himself landed with Phillips, the Marine officer, and nine Marines, covered by the *Resolution*'s launch (under the command of Lt. John Williamson, R.N.).

Finding that the king could not be induced to come aboard peaceably, and that the natives were in an ugly mood, Cook gave up the attempt to procure hostages, and started back to the beach. At this moment, news came that a chief had been shot by one of the boats of the cordon. A fight broke out between the landing-party and the natives; the latter stood a volley of musketry composedly, and rushed the landing-place while their opponents were struggling to re-load.

Four of the Marines were killed, and three others, with Phillips, dangerously wounded. Cook, when last seen, was standing at the water's edge, calling to the boats to cease firing, and pull in. While so engaged, he was stabbed in the back, and fell on his face in the water, where he was held down – being afterwards hauled ashore and butchered.[1]

The whole affair was a tragedy of errors – a miserable, stupid blunder. The natives seem to have had no feelings of animosity against Cook – as soon as the excitement had died down they showed themselves most sincerely sorry for what had happened. Friendly relations were resumed before the ships left.

That a man so experienced in dealing with the Pacific islanders should end his life so tragically, has always seemed remarkable. Needless to say, the 'unco' guid' – and even such normally charitable men as Cowper, the poet – have not been slow in ascribing the event to Providence, outraged by Cook's accepting the worship offered him by the natives. There is no real evidence that he did this – but, if he considered that complying with the native beliefs would promote the execution of his duty, what sensible man would blame him for complying? Such an attitude of mind recalls Stevenson's 'Bottle-Imp', and the tale that the San Franciscan told:

> ... Napoleon had this bottle, and by it he grew to be the king of the world; but he sold it at the last, and fell. Captain Cook had this bottle, and by it he found his way to so many islands; but he, too, sold it, and was slain upon Hawaii. For, once it is sold, the power goes, and the protection ...

[1] Editor's note: here I disagree with Gould's summary of events. See Gavin Kennedy, *The Death of Captain Cook*, London 1978.

Cook's Death — and After

Actually, Cook's end was due to an error of judgement such as even the greatest men must sometimes make. He had often before put his plan of seizing hostages into practice; and its result had been uniformly successful. Also, he had always found that natives, however brave, were over-awed by the concerted use of firearms – and it was the shock, so contrary to his men's experience, of finding the Hawaiians undeterred by their volley which undermined their morale and led directly to their being overpowered.

The darkest spot in the whole tragedy is the behaviour of Williamson, the lieutenant in charge of the launch. He made no attempt to go to Cook's help, and his boat never fired a shot. Clerke, who succeeded Cook in the command, was in poor health (he died of consumption the same year, near Petropavlosk) and did not bring him to a court-martial; but it is worth noting that Williamson, when a Captain, was tried for cowardice after Camperdown, and cashiered. Yet I do not think he acted from cowardice on this occasion. It will be remembered that he had had to shoot a native at Nihau; and his journal of the event suggests that he was no coward, but a good deal of a prig. He notes:

> (The) different opinions Capt. Cook & I held on this matter, made me request him never to send me on duty where I could not act from reason & ye dictates of my own Conscience.

Obviously, Williamson was the last man in the world to put in charge of an armed boat if there were any chance of the latter coming into conflict with the natives. He could, as he showed, lie by and see his captain and other men, hopelessly outnumbered, fight for their lives and ultimately be butchered within a stone's throw of him, and yet not lift a finger to save them or to let others save them. Of all normally good men, the high-principled fanatic can, on occasion, be the cruellest – and such a man, I think, was Williamson. At all events, whether he were fanatic or coward, Cook's death must lie at his door.

On February 22, having recovered most of Cook's remains and given them burial at sea, the ships left to complete their programme as far as possible. Gore was now in command of the *Discovery*, and Clerke of the *Resolution*; but his ill-health put the conduct of the ships largely into the capable hands of Bligh, the *Resolution*'s Master. Calling at Petropavlosk, they re-passed Bering Strait, but were again stopped by ice in 70° 33' N. (July 19, 1779); and after fruitless attempts to force a passage they made for Petropavlosk. Clerke died the day before their arrival, and was buried there. He was only thirty-seven, and had been with Cook in all three voyages. Gore returned to the *Resolution*, and King took command of the *Discovery*. After sighting the eastern coast of Japan, they reached Macao on December 1, and the Cape of Good Hope on April 11, 1780 – thus returning along their outward route, without circumnavigating the globe. On October 4, 1780, they arrived off the Nore, having been absent over four years.

News of Cook's death had already reached England (January 10, 1780) having been sent overland by Clerke from Petropavlosk. The regret and interest it aroused was widespread; for since Cook's departure from England in 1776 many events had shown that his reputation had spread far beyond the borders of his own country. In particular, both France and the United States (then at war with Britain) had unofficially recommended to their ships that, if they fell in with Cook's expedition, they were not only to abstain from offensive action but to offer him any assistance in their power. The Royal

Society, too, had awarded him the highest honour in its gift – the Copley Medal – for his methods of preventing scurvy; and in 1777 his journal of the second voyage (edited by Canon Douglas) had told the story of that great achievement in clear, simple and seamanlike language. If Cook had returned, there is some ground for thinking that George III would have made him a baronet. As matters stood, his wife received a grant of arms – an unusual honour – a special pension of £200 a year, and the right to a share in the profits arising from the publication of her husband's journals. The Royal Society struck a special medal in Cook's honour, and Banks – now Sir Joseph Banks, its president, but still proud to style himself Cook's friend – forwarded an example to Mrs. Cook with an expression of the whole Society's regret for her loss: an expression which was much more than a formality. And the years were to bring her many tributes which, I think, she valued even more highly: the published testimony of those explorers, of all nations, who were to follow in her husband's tracks and to realise – as few others could realise – the vastness of his accomplished work and the amazing standard which he had set.

She survived him in comfortable circumstances more than fifty years, dying in 1835 at the age of ninety-three. Unhappily, all her six children had long been dead. Three died in infancy; her second son, Nathaniel, went down in the *Thunderer*, off Jamaica, in the same week that the *Resolution* and *Discovery* reached the Nore; in December, 1793, her youngest son, Hugh, died of scarlet fever at Cambridge; and five weeks afterwards her eldest boy, James Cook the younger, Commander R.N., was either drowned or murdered while sailing from Poole to Portsmouth. There is a vague tradition that this son was married (shortly before his death) at Huntingdon, and had issue; but this is entirely unsubstantiated. So far as is known, no direct descendants of Cook were alive fifteen years after his death.

Of Cook himself, many appreciations have been written. King, who completed the official account of the last voyage, wrote a noble tribute based upon personal knowledge – and there have been many others since. But, to my mind, one of the most striking of all is to be found in a little book published at Mannheim, two years after Cook's death, by Heinrich Zimmermann, a German who was coxswain of the *Discovery* during the last voyage. Zimmermann's point of view is as far removed from that of an official account as the foc'sle is from the poop; moreover, he was a foreigner on foreign soil, owing no allegiance either to England or Hanover, and it would have been easy and safe for him to vent any private spite against his late commander, or to make his book a *chronique scandaleuse.* Yet while he honestly sets down the one defect in Cook's character – his hasty temper – he has left us, nevertheless, a sincere and an obviously faithful portrait of a man who was really great. He dwells upon Cook's insistence on scrupulous cleanliness, the strict but just discipline he kept, his moderation ('. . . throughout the entire voyage, no one ever saw him drunk'), his unvarying personal chastity among temptations to which all others gave way, his personal courage, his incessant care for his ship and his men, and his talent for winning and keeping the respect – and often the affection – of the natives. This is the unsolicited and gratuitous tribute of a humble German seaman; and, to my mind, it is worth all the floods of official eulogy poured forth on the occasion of Cook's bi-centenary, and the sesqui-centenary of his discovery of Hawaii, in 1928.

Yet such occasions have their use, apart from the opportunities of self-advertisement that they give to those who exploit them. To be remembered by name after the lapse of two centuries – still more, to be remembered with honour – falls to the lot of very few. Most men rest assured that in much less than two centuries no one alive will know, or care, that they have ever been. Only to a handful comes that strange, intangible thing which men call Fame – and none can ever be certain, in his lifetime, that he stands among them. Many who would give – who have given – their lives for fame, have failed to achieve it: some who have snatched at it too eagerly have found that, once in their grasp, it was not fame but infamy: and those who have won it have never, I think, consciously aimed at it, but have been content simply to do their duty, as they saw it, in accordance with a self-set standard too high for their fellows. Such men are the true salt of the earth – and such a man, beyond all question, was James Cook.

Index

Abraham, Heights of, 23
Admiralty Bay, N.Z., 63
Adventure, 77, 105
Alarm, 21
Aleutian Is., 102, 115
Amherst, Gen. Jeffrey, 24
Amsterdam Is., 88
Amundsen, Roald, 107
Anderson, Surgeon, 106, 109, 114
Animals, shipped on third voyage, 106, 107, 110
Anson, Lord, 47
Antarctic Circle, 31, 85, 89
Antelope, 21, 25
Antipodes Is., 89
Arctic Circle, 104
Arnold, John, 80
Australia, 43, 65
'Austrialia del Spiritu Santo', 91
Ayton, Yorkshire, 16

Baffin Bay, 102, 106
Baltic Sea, 17
Banks, Sir Joseph, 40, 52, 69, 78, 82, 121
Banks Peninsular, 62
Barrington, Hon. Daines, 101
barter with Tahitians, rules for, 52
Bass Rock, 20; Strait, 66, 87
Batavia, 59, 66, 72
Batts, Miss Elizabeth, 24; as Cook's wife, 121
Bayly, William, 80, 105
Beaufoy, 89
Bellingshausen, Russian explorer, 96
Benkulen, Sumatra, 29
Bering, Veit, 102, 114
Bering Strait, 102, 114, 120
Bevis, Dr. John, 27
Bird, instrument maker, 27
Bisset, Master of *Eagle*, 21
Bligh, Capt., 72, 105, 120
Borabora, 111
Boscawen, Adl. Edward, 21
Boston, New England, 104
Botany Bay, 67
'Bottle-Imp', 118
Bougainville, L. A. de, 51, 57, 92, 111
Bounty, 72, 105
Bouvet Is., 97

Bouvet de Lozier, J. B. C., 76, 84
'British Mariners' Guide', 46
Buache, geographer, 32
Buchan, artist on first voyage, 41, 53
Burgeo Is., Newfoundland, 26
Burney, James, 112
Byron, Commodore, 35, 50, 82

Campbell, geographer, 102
Camperdown, 119
Canada, French possessions in, 34
Cape Circumcision, 76, 84, 93, 95; as Bouvet Is., 97
Cape (of Good Hope): first voyage, 30, 43, 64, 73; second voyage, 83; third voyage, 106, 120
Cape Horn: first voyage, 43, 50, 64; second voyage, 76, 94
Carbonera Bay, 24
Carruthers, Sir Joseph, 44
Carteret, Capt., 35, 51, 82
Chapeau Rouge, Cape, 27
Chirikov, 102
Christmas Is., 111; Sound, 94
chronometers in actual service, 80
Clerke, Charles, 105, 107, 119
Columbus, Christopher, 15
Colville, Capt. Lord, 23
Cook, Capt. James: early life, 16; enrols in R.N., 18; 'Master R.N.,' 20; marries, 24; children, 25, 26, 121; personal accidents, 26; appears before Royal Society Council, 38; describes Antarctic scene, 90; presented to George III, 100; death, 118; tributes to, 122 *see also,* scurvy; surveys by Cook
Cook Inlet, 114; Island, 109; Strait, 62, 88
Cook's Passage, 70
Cooktown, 70
Cooper, Lieut., 79
Cowper, William, 118
crossing the line, 48
Crozet, French explorer, 63, 83, 106
Crozet Is., 86, 108
Cuba, 34

Dahlgren, 112

Index

Dalrymple, Alexander, 32, 60, 65, 75, 93
Dalrymple's 'Continent', *see* Great Southern Continent
D'Apres de Mannevillette, geographer, 32
date-line, 59
dating systems, used in ships' logs, 58
Davis, explorer, 33, 91
De Brosse, geographer, 32
de Fonte, 104
de Fuca, Juan, 104, 113
Delisle, J. N., 30, 104
Denia Is., 97
Deshnef, Cape, 102
de Surville, 62
Discovery, 105
Dolphin, 35, 57
Douglas, Rev. John, 101
Drake, Sir Francis, 102
Duc D'Aquitaine, 20
Durell, Adl., 22
Dusky Bay, N.Z., 87
Dutch East Indies, 66

Eagle, 18
East Cape, 102
Easter Is., 91
East India Company, 36
eclipse of the sun, 26
Efate, New Hebrides, 112
Encke, Johann Franz, 55
Endeavour, 16; commanded by Cook, 38; description of, 40; nearly lost on a reef, 68; deaths on board, 72; sold out of the Navy, 77
Erebus, 85

Falkland Is., 35, 93
Fernandez, Juan, 33, 91
Ferrol point, St John's, 26
Fishburn of Whitby, Messrs., 39, 77
Florida, 34
Forster, John Reingold, 80, 83, 91, 101
Fort Venus, 53, 88
France, territories occupied by, 34
Freelove, collier, 17
Friendly Is., 88
Friendship, 17
Funchal, Madeira, 48
Furneaux, Tobias, 78, 86, 93, 105

Gaetano, Juan, 112
Gallipoli, attack on Quebec compared with, 22
Garland, 20
George III, 55, 100, 121
Golden Hind, 78

Good Success Bay, 50
Gore, Lieut., 53, 63, 105, 120
Gosport, 24
Grampus, 20
Graves, Capt., 25
Great Barrier Reef, 70
Great Southern Continent, 31, 57, 74, 91
Green, Charles, 39, 46, 70, 80, 82
Greenwich, 26; time, 45
Greenwich Hospital, 100
Grenville, 25, 38
'Gulf of San Sebastian', 93
Gvosdev, explorer, 102, 114

Hailes, Lord, 32
Halifax, Nova Scotia, 21
Halley, Edmund, 28, 97
Hamar, Captain of *Eagle*, 19
Harbour Grace, 24
Hardy, Sir Charles, 22
Harrison, John, 46, 80, 105
Hawaii, 115
Hawke, Lord, 36
Hawkesworth, Dr John, 82, 100
Hazard, 21
Heard Is., 86
Hearne, Samuel, 104
Hell, Father, 55
Hervey Is., 88, 109
Hicks, Lieut., 48, 53, 73
Hodges, William, 80
Huahine, Soc. Is., 111
Hudson Bay, 29, 99, 102, 106
Humboldt, Baron von, 112
Hydrographic Dept., 27

Ile d'Orléans, 22
India, French possessions in, 34
'Instructions' issued to Cook: first voyage, 42; second voyage, 76, 85; third voyage, 106
Isla de San Pedro, 95
Ismailov, Russian trader, 115
'Israelites', 107

Jane, 89
Japan, 120
Johnson, Dr. Samuel, 82
Jupiter, first satellite of, 70

Kamchatka, 102
Kangaroo, Great, 70
Kauai Is., 112
Kealakekua Bay, 116
Kenai peninsular, 114
Kendall, Larcum, 81, 105
Kerguelen Is., 86, 108

Kerguelen-Tremarec, 75, 83, 106
King, 2nd Lieut., 105, 109, 117
King George III Is. (Tahiti), 40
Kippis, Dr. Andrew, 20
Kitson, 21, 42
Krech, sailor in *Valdivia*, 97
Kronenberg, 72

La Boudeuse, 57
Land's End, 73
Lane, Michael, 16, 27, 38
Lark, 26
La Roche, Antonio, 95
Le Gentil, French traveller, 54
Leith, 20
Le Maire Strait, 50
Leon, 76, 93
L'Etoile, 57
Lima, 110
Lind, Dr., 78
Lindsay, sealer, 97
Linnaeus, Carl, botanist, 83
Lizard Pt., 73
longitude, determined by Cook, 26; problems of determining, 45
Lorient, 75
Louisberg, 21
Low Archipelago, 40, 88
Lowthian-Green, 31

Macao, 120
Madeira, 77, 82, 106
Magellan, Ferdinand, 15
Magellan Strait, 50
Manila, 65
Maoris, language understood by Tupia, 60; suspicious of Cook, 108
'Maria van Diemen, Cape', 62
Marion, French explorer, 83, 108
Marquesas Islands, 33, 91
Marseveen Is., 97
Martinique, 34
Marton in Cleveland, 16
Mary, 17
Maskelyne, Nevil, 30, 46, 55
'Master, R.N.', description of office, 19
Matavai Bay, Tahiti, 51, 57, 88, 110
Maui Is., 115
Mauritius, 75
Mayflower, 78
Mendana, explorer, 33, 91
Mercury, 20
Middleburg Is., 88
Mile End, home of Cook, 101
Miquelon, Newfoundland, 25
Molineux, Robert, 51, 73
Monkhouse, surgeon, 50, 52
Montagu, John, 112

Morrell, sealer, 97
Morton, Lord, 37
Muller, explorer, 102

'Nautical Almanac', 46
'Naval Miscellany', 42
Navy Board, 78
'New Albion', 103; coast of, 106
New Caledonia, 92
Newfoundland, 22
New France, 21
New Guinea, 65
New Hebrides, 92
New Holland, 43, 65
New South Wales, 72, 105
'New Wales', 72
New Zealand, 44, 86, 93, 106; reached on first voyage, 58
'Nieuw Zeeland', 33
Nihau Is., 112
Nootka Sound, 113
Nordenskjöld, Baron, 107
Nore, 79, 120
Norris, sealer, 97
North America, western coast, 102
North American Squadron, 23
North-East Passage, 107
Northumberland, 23
North-West Passage, 99, 104
Norton Sound, 115

Oahu Is., 112
Omai, Tahitian, 105, 110
Orange Tree, 33, 51
Ortelius, Abraham, 93
Osbaldestone, Mr., 20

pack-ice, 84, 89
Palliser, Capt. Hugh, 20, 79, 105
Paramour, 36
Paris, Treaty of, 25, 34
Parkinson, artist on first voyage, 41, 73
Patten, ship's surgeon, 91
Pelsart, traveller, 70
Pembroke, 21, 47
Petropavlovsk, 115, 120
Philippine Is., 34
Phillips, Marine officer, 117
'Philosophical Transactions', 27
Pitcairn Is., 51, 88
Plymouth, 20, 74, 82, 106
'Point Hicks', 66
Pondicherry, 54
Poole, 121
Portsmouth, 18
Prince Edward Is., 108
Prince of Wales, Cape, 114
Prince William Sound, 114

Index

Privy Purse, grant from, 37, 55
promotion, in R.N., 18
Ptolemy, Greek philosopher, 31
Puget sound, 113

Quebec, 22
Queen Charlotte's Sound, 62, 87, 92, 108
Quiros, explorer, 33, 66, 91

Resolution, 77, 105
Reynolds, artist on first voyage, 41, 73
Rio de Janeiro, 48
Roggeveen, explorer, 91
Rose, 39
Ross, Capt. James Clark, 85, 97
Royal Society, 27, 35, 57, 121
Russian traders, 115

St. Elias, Mount, 102, 113
St. Helena, 46
St. Jean Baptiste, 62
St. John's, Newfoundland, 24
St. Lawrence: Basin, 23; Gulf of, 21; River, 22
St. Petersburg Academy of Sciences, 103
St. Philip and St. James, bay, 92
St. Pierre, Newfoundland, 25
Sanderson, grocer at Staithes, 17
Sandwich, Lord, 101, 105
Sandwich Is., 112
'Sandwich Land', 96
Santa Cruz, harbour, 92
Saunders, Adl. Sir Charles, 22
Savu, 72
Schiehallion, 56
Scorpion, 78
scurvy, avoidance of, 47, 51, 82, 87; Royal Society award, 121
Seven Years War, 19, 34, 54
Shadwell, 24
Ship Cove, N.Z., 62
Short, James, 54
Smart, assistant surveyor, 25
Society Is., 57, 88, 106
Solander, Dr., botanist, 41, 73, 78, 82
Solebay, 20
Southern Continent, *see* Great Southern Continent
'Southern Thule', 96
South Georgia, 95
South Indian Ocean, 75, 93
South Orkneys, 93
South Shetlands, 93
Spain, territories occupied by, 34
Sparrman, Anders, 83
Spithead, 93

Spöring, naturalist, 41
Staithes, 17
Staten Is., 50
Stephens, secretary, 105
Stewart Is., 63
Stoehlin, geographer, 103, 107, 114
Stone, astronomer, 55
'Strait of Anian', 104
surveys by Cook: St. Lawrence Basin, 23; Harbour Grace and Carbonera Bay, 24; Newfoundland, 25; Society Is., 57; coastline of New Zealand, 63; NW coast of North America, 113
Swallow, 35

Tahiti, 40, 49, 106, 109; Cook arrives on first voyage, 51; second voyage, 88; third voyage, 110
Tasman, Abel Janszoon, 33, 44, 58, 60, 75
Tasmania, 65, 76, 86
Terror, 85
thefts by Tahitians, 53, 111
Three Brothers, 17
'Three Kings Is.', 62
Thunderer, 121
Tierra del Fuego, 50, 94
Tonga Is., 88
Torres Strait, 66
Tryal, 39
Tupia, Tahitian pilot, 57, 73
Turnagain, Cape, 61
Tweed, 25

Unalaska, 115

Vaez de Torres, Luis, 65
Vahitahi, atoll, 51
Valdivia, 97
Vancouver, George, 104
Vancouver Is., 113
'Van Diemen's Land', 65; *and see* Tasmania
van Plettenburg, Baron, 83
venereal disease on Tahiti, 56
Venus, transit of, 28; witnessed by Cook, 54; missed by Le Gentil, 54
Vespucci, Amerigo, 95
Victoria and Albert, 79
Victory, 78

Wales, William, 80
Walker, John, of Whitby, 17, 100
Wallis, Capt., 35, 51, 78, 82, 110
Wardhuus, Lapland, 55
Webber, artist, 106
Weddell, James, 89
Wharton, Admiral, 42

Whitby, 17
White, Sir William, 79
Wilkes, Lieut. Charles, 80
Williamson, Lieut. John, 113, 117, 119
Wolfe, James, 22

York, Cape, 65; Island, 53

Zimmermann, Heinrich, 122
Zoffany, John, 78
Zone Time, 59